Claiming
EARTH as
Common Ground

The
Ecological Crisis
through the
Lens of Faith

276271

Andrea Cohen-Kiener

Foreword by Rev. Sally Bingham

Walking Together, Finding the Way®
SKYLIGHT PATHS®
PUBLISHING
Woodstock, Vermont

Claiming Earth as Common Ground:
The Ecological Crisis through the Lens of Faith

2009 Quality Paperback Edition, First Printing
© 2009 by Andrea Cohen-Kiener
Foreword © 2009 by Sally Bingham

Scripture quotations marked NRSV are from the *New Revised Standard Version Bible,* copyright © 1989 by the Division of Christian Education of the National Council of the Churches of Christ in the USA. Used by permission. All rights reserved.

All other scripture translations are by the author.

A Note from the Author: I refer to the scripture of Judaism as *First Testament* because this reflects my understanding of the position of Hebrew Scriptures better than the phrase *Old Testament* does. I refer to the exclusively Christian foundational texts as the *Second Testament.*

Page 176 constitutes a continuation of this copyright page.

Library of Congress Cataloging-in-Publication Data
Cohen-Kiener, Andrea.
   Claiming earth as common ground : the ecological crisis through the lens of faith / Andrea Cohen-Kiener ; foreword by Sally Bingham.—Quality paperback ed.
      p. cm.
   Includes bibliographical references.
   ISBN-13: 978-1-59473-261-4 (quality pb original)
   ISBN-10: 1-59473-261-2 (quality pb original)   1. Human ecology—Religious aspects—Christianity. 2. Ecotheology. I. Title.
   BT695.5.C645 2009
   261.8'8—dc22

                                                                              2009011573

10   9   8   7   6   5   4   3   2   1
Manufactured in the United States of America
Cover design: Jenny Buono

SkyLight Paths Publishing is creating a place where people of different spiritual traditions come together for challenge and inspiration, a place where we can help each other understand the mystery that lies at the heart of our existence.

SkyLight Paths sees both believers and seekers as a community that increasingly transcends traditional boundaries of religion and denomination—people wanting to learn from each other, *walking together, finding the way.*

Walking Together, Finding the Way®
Published by SkyLight Paths Publishing
A Division of Longhill Partners, Inc.
Sunset Farm Offices, Route 4, P.O. Box 237
Woodstock, VT 05091
Tel: (802) 457-4000   Fax: (802) 457-4004
www.skylightpaths.com

This book is dedicated to the founding board of the Inter-religious Eco-Justice Network: Lynn Fulkerson, David Barrett, and Rev. Tom Carr. The organization they formed has been a catalyst for environmental activism in Connecticut and beyond. Their steady vision and commitment have caused earth stewardship to flourish in many forms. Their mentoring of and partnership with me have been a source of new relationships and new insights. I am grateful to them for opening many doors.

CONTENTS

Foreword ix
   by Rev. Sally Bingham

Introduction 1

1 ❧ **The Making of an Environmental Activist:**
Waking Up to the Problem   7
   The Terrible Contradiction 7
   Too Good to Be True! 10
   The Spiritual Challenge of a Mountain of Garbage .13
   Agents for Transformation 15
   The Ultimate Common Ground 18

2 ❧ **The Makings of a Movement:**
The Interfaith Imperative and Its Obstacles   21
   The Mountain of God 21
   Obstacles on the Path 22
   God of the Pews or God of the Cosmos? 25
   Leaving Base Camp 28
   The One about the Rabbi and the Evangelical 36
   Getting above the Tree Line 40

3 ⸙ **The New Wealth: Spirit Matters**   43

    What Is Enough? 43

    Old Models for New Wealth 44

    A Living Vision 47

    Tools We Bring to the Table 50

    Transforming Business as Usual 53

    Imagine the Alternatives 56

4 ⸙ **Working Beyond Class and Race:**
    Yes, We Do Need to Do This Together   59

    We Need to Talk 59

    Getting Beyond "Over There" 60

    Finding Common Cause 63

    Working Together 65

    ✒ THE GREAT LIGHT BULB SWAP OF '06 66
       by Rev. Woody Bartlett

    Getting to the Table 73

5 ⸙ **How Big Is Your God?**
    Theology Meets Earth-Care Activism   77

    Digging Deeper 77

    ✒ THE BIG CONTEXT 79
       by Rev. Tom Carr

6 ⸙ **The New Eden: Reclaiming the Garden**   93

    Seeds of Possibility 93

    ✒ WHEAT SHEAVES AND MATZA TALES 97
       by Elisheva Rogosa

    ✒ COMMUNION AGRICULTURE 101
       by Andrea Ferich

Contents

7 ⌁ The New Sabbath: Less Is More   115

    Unnamed Hungers 115

    ✍ GREEN SABBATH 119
        by Rev. Donna Schaper, PhD

    Creating New Sabbath Rituals 125

8 ⌁ Eco-Conversion: A New Paradigm for a New Earth   129

    Seeing with Green Eyes 129

    ✍ CONVERSION TO ECO-JUSTICE 130
        by Rev. Margaret Bullitt-Jonas, PhD

    The Power of Witnessing 137

    Going Forward 141

Appendix I
Many Small Steps   146

Appendix II
Creating a Sustainable Civilization:
Joanna Macy's Theoretical Foundations   150

Appendix III
Thoughts for Discussion and Action:
Format for an Eight-week Study Session   153

Appendix IV
Interfaith Ecological Resources   162

Acknowledgments   169

About the Contributors   171

FOREWORD

WE ARE FEELING CHANGE ALL AROUND US. Change is in the air. Not only climate change, but also social and economic change. The age that we are entering is going to be one of more progressive thinking—one where religion will change, too. I expect to see faith in action taking the place of ancient ritual, liturgy, and focus on the past. Religion, like everything else, will need to focus on the future if it wants to continue to be a relevant voice in society. If it can do that, religion may once again be a strong voice in finding solutions to some of societies' major problems. But to do so, religion must speak out on issues that are relevant to today's needs, and we must provide the hope that is sorely missing from the scientific message of environmental catastrophe.

For the past two decades, young people have been seen less and less in congregations. This may be due largely to the lack of relevance that today's youth find when they visit the congregation of their parents. This may change with the forward and creative thinking of many religious leaders who have themselves awakened to the realization that God's very creation is threatened and, without intervention, may no longer be able to support the human species. We know we need to change our behavior and attitude toward the environment—perhaps even create a new identity of what it means to be human today on a planet that we have wasted.

We know we need to change direction from our focus on consumption to something more sustainable. And we are beginning to realize that the moral voice of religion *must* play a role in making these changes become a reality.

Most mainstream religions teach us to be the stewards of creation, and many of us have come to understand that putting faith into action is the only way we will save ourselves from ourselves and prevent catastrophic disruption. Many religious leaders have come to recognize this urgent call to mobilize and work across denominational divides—to stand in solidarity in an effort to save our fragile earth from complete destruction. Rabbi Andrea Cohen-Kiener is one such leader. She recognizes the importance of working not only with other organizations, such as science and labor and business, but also with other religions. If divided, we will not be able to make the major changes we need to make. However, if all major religions reach out to each other in solidarity, we can be a powerful force.

Ecology and theology have only recently become intertwined. It was at the invitation of the scientific community in 1991 that many of us became aware of what humans were doing to the planet. It was at a meeting in Washington, D.C., hosted by Al Gore and attended by many of the twentieth-century's best-known scientists such as Carl Sagan and Stephen Schneider, that religious leaders from all over the country were brought to their knees. The evidence of destruction to our life-sustaining ecosystem, and the sincere pleading from the scientists for religion to rethink its relationship with science, was overwhelming. They were pleading for our help in finding solutions that would turn the tide of destruction of the earth to one of regeneration and reconciliation. They were asking us to be pro-life in the very broadest sense of the imagination. Science can and did give us the facts, outlining the end result of our continued lack of appreciation for how fragile the earth is.

That was almost two decades ago, and we have been slow to respond. Science says it's not too late, but the situation is urgent and we need to act. Now is the time for religion to play its part in helping to transform thinking and implement heartfelt changes in behavior. We cannot wait any longer if we want to leave behind a world that our children can enjoy.

Recognizing that we need the help of the moral authority that religion brings, Andrea and her fellow writers have collaborated in *Claiming Earth as Common Ground* to present a wake-up call. They acknowledge the challenges of working in an interfaith environment, but they also celebrate the collaboration that shared values bring. They openly share their experiences not only of how their personal faith impels them, but of how the values they hold in common with different faith traditions deepens their own faith. We all have far more in common than we have differences, and the commonalities we share are never more poignant than the earth itself.

With her keen wit, humor, and passion for saving creation, Andrea has produced a powerful and important piece of literature. She has found her voice and her self-expression in *Claiming Earth as Common Ground*—it will move you. She will enlighten you with reasons for changing and inspire you to do so. She will demonstrate for you that the old way of religion is changing, too. Values that interpret human relationship to nature are changing out of the realization that we are slowly but determinedly destroying the very thing that was given to sustain us. The once deeply rooted belief that, as humans, we could never harm God's creation has been replaced by a keen awareness that actually we have and are destroying our life-support system.

We need to stop this behavior, and soon. One by one, people like Andrea and I—one rabbi and one priest among many—are working together to be agents of change, and to save both the planet and the valuable voice of religion in everyday life. We can and we will. But we must all work together. It is the only way.

—Rev. Sally Bingham,
founder and president,
Interfaith Power and Light

INTRODUCTION

EVERY ONE OF US IS AN INDIVIDUAL with a unique personal trajectory through this life. Yet each of us has a shared heritage of earth, and our common fate is tied to this heritage. It is more and more apparent that our collective impact on this planet will cause disruption to the life-giving capacity of earth for generations to come—unless we act.

A hundred years ago, it was impossible—even arrogant—to imagine that humans could have an impact on the planet. Now our impact is impossible to ignore. There is a shift in the temperature, the wind, and the forests. There are disturbing changes in the sea, the fauna, and the rain. There are many of us, and our impact touches the very physics of creation. All this is new.

In the shared religious tradition of the Abrahamic faiths, God says to the suffering Job, "Where were you when I set the limit of the sea?" And in our time, we, the children of Job, are contributing to a rise in sea level. The book of Numbers foretells that straying from our right desires will not only lead to acid rain, infertility, weather aberrations, and illness, but that a distortion of our spirit will lead to a distortion in our environment (Job 38:10). The Qur'an teaches the same thing: "And in the earth are portents for those whose faith is sure, And (also) in yourselves. Can ye then not see?" (Sura 51:20–21, translation by M. Pickthall). We are each a microcosmos, a small world. Signs in our very nature teach us about the imprint of the Creator upon us. When we ourselves become distorted, we will see distortions in the earth systems that sustain us. The environmental problems we face are, in part, the symptoms of a spiritual crisis.

I have written this book to encourage people of faith to address this question: Can religious people save the environment? And I have discovered along the way that there is a second and equally important question to be addressed: Can the environmental challenge save religion?

Episcopal, Catholic, Baptist, Muslim, Jew—one after another have told me that if our faith cannot help us address this deepest threat to our shared future, religion is a relic and not worth our time. And yet the colleagues have also told me that reading their traditions' stories "with green eyes" opened their faith to them, and enriched their relationship with God, in new and powerful ways.

I hope that an army of people of every creed and sect will read this book and renew their commitment to their own faith traditions. And I hope that they will reclaim their mandate to care for creation as a core expression of their faith. As people of faith, we have the numbers, the credibility, and the influence to be agents of change. If we can train our lights together on the care of creation, we may be able to bequeath to future generations the opportunity to sustain the human project on earth.

I do not think God is done with us. But I think our current course—of economy, of appetite—imperils us. I think the human project will continue, but it may be in smaller numbers and in scattered locations. I know that the current strain of agriculture and transportation and heating and illumination of our lifestyle is not sustainable with current technologies. It is up to us whether we choose our way out of the bind or whether we allow the inevitable consequences of climate change and resource wars to overwhelm us.

Can the religious save the environment? Can people of faith organize and act in sufficient numbers, with a deep enough impact, to transform our economy and our values as a culture?

And can environment save religion? Can the shared concerns of the human project on earth trump the creedal and denominational interests we hold? Can we see our way past our denominational boundaries into a project of earth care that builds our compassion, our mutual self-interest, and our devotion to going forward together as a species?

As director of an interfaith project—the Interreligious Eco-Justice Network, the Connecticut affiliate of Interfaith Power and Light—I have had ample opportunity to confront the issues that beset us. I have met people of every creed and race who understand the challenge we face at this juncture in human history. And I have learned from their stories what it takes to become a compassionate and passionate advocate of earth stewardship. I am privileged to count these people as my allies and my friends. I have seen the challenge of environmental destruction as an opportunity to know and work with my fellows in deeper and truer ways, even as I walk my path as a Jew and they walk theirs as Catholic, as Muslim, as Protestant, and on and on.

What a challenge and an opportunity we have!

In this book, I have tried to be truthful. I have tried to move myself and others beyond the platitudes of our glorious religious expressions and into the nitty-gritty, the difficult challenges of forging effective partnerships for environmental activism. The time for platitudes is past. It is time to work together, with a dedication to our true common interests. Even when serious doctrinal issues divide us, such as the pros and cons of what role human population plays in the environmental crisis—an unbridgeable gap between Catholic and non-Catholic communities—we have refused to let the dialogue stop there. We have kept our sights on what can be shared. We have continued to see the common ground.

The contributors to this volume have shared their pride in and affiliation with their faith tradition. They have also spoken truthfully about their personal and collective struggle to live the earth-stewardship values espoused by the holy books. I hope that this truthfulness will make *Claiming Earth as Common Ground* a helpful book as you work within your own faith community, and through interfaith efforts, to embody your commitment to care for creation.

In the opening pages of the book, I speak in personal ways about what it was like to become aware of the enormity of the problem. And then, in each chapter, my contributors and I tackle some of the obstacles to the work we believe is both timely and necessary. We write about the deleterious handmaidens of classism and racism and try to see how these two *isms* operate together to untangle our necessary partnerships. We reflect on the spiritual, theological, and psychological issues of coming together as different faith communities. We try to create a common language and find a way to overcome the obstacles we name. We pay special attention to the story of food. How we nourish ourselves has changed so much, leaving an indelible mark on the landscape, as well as on our communities and our economies. We recognize that we will need to reclaim the original human task of gardener in a new and sustainable way. We acknowledge that we can solve these problems in the material realm only if we undergo a spiritual transformation.

In the end, we come back to the question of our humanness— our needs and our urges and our desires. What do we truly need to be safe and happy and healthy? To have the abundance of the land burst forth in front of us and watch our children grow old—this is the simple promise of Deuteronomy (11:21).

At the close of the book, I have provided a series of "Thoughts for Discussion and Action" for your continuing study. The work of claiming earth as common ground is transformative, and the insights take time to integrate. We must increase our capacity for honest dialogue and collective action. I hope the study guide will encourage individuals and groups to continue the conversation. I urge you to consider gathering a small group from your church or synagogue or mosque for an eight-week study session to explore together your perspective and your role in this important work of creation care.

Humanity is facing a collective brush with mortality. It is time for us to reflect, as Noah did before the cataclysm in his time, on what we truly need. In the face of this sobering challenge, we must look toward a new beginning and make it a reality.

Environmental problem solving usually encompasses some element of self-denial, of less. I believe that if we rebalance our spiritual and material hungers, our environmental repair may yield a time of more—much more: more connections, more wisdom, and more abundance. I invite all hands on deck to steer the ship around this iceberg and set sail for a safer harbor.

THE EARTH IS ALIVE

The Earth is Alive and she breathes.
The winds of the world and the leaves of the
    vegetation;
The gills of fish and the brachia of all species, these
    are the breath of the Earth.

The Earth is Alive and she eats.
The bacteria of the soil and the guts of worms;
The teeth and flesh and bowels of all life, these are
    the digestive tract of the Earth.

The Earth is Alive and she has a circulatory system.
The waterways and aquifers, the clouds and the rain,
The pulse and blood of all life—these are the circu-
    latory system of the Earth.

The Earth is Alive and she knows.
The nervous system of all beings,
The frontal lobes of higher mammals,
These are Earth's capacity to know herself.
We are the thought of the Earth.

The Earth is Alive and she breathes.
The exhaust of our engines and the fumes of our
    garbage heaps;
The scarred and cancer-filled lungs of all life, these
    are the breath of the Earth.

The Earth is Alive and she eats.
The diminished range of species and the engineered
    seeds,
Captive livestock and roadside carrion, these are the
    digestive system of the Earth.

The Earth is Alive and she has a circulatory system.
The Drano and detergent in our drains,
The acid and metals in our gentle rain, these infuse
    the bloodstream of the Earth.

The Earth is Alive and she thinks.
The discomfort in our guts,
The ache of our spirits,
The desolation of our disconnection—
These are Earth's capacity to know herself.
We are the thought of the Earth.

1

The Making of an Environmental Activist

Waking Up to the Problem

THE TERRIBLE CONTRADICTION

WHEN I WAS A YOUNG CHILD, there was talk about the end of life as we know it. Sometime around third grade, we were allowed to come out from under our desks and the Threat of Communism, only to be greeted by overpopulation, followed by pollution, and now global warming. I am not sure whether previous generations had to endure the thought that we could blink ourselves out of existence, but this terrifying possibility has been the backdrop of our lives for two generations now.

What do we do? We sneeze. We get asthma and cancer. And we treat these illnesses with medicines and procedures that deepen and worsen the problem. We imagine that these diseases are personal shortcomings or challenges, not environmental epidemics. We try to move to a "nice area" with more parks and less blight. We thank our lucky stars we do not live in the "City" or the Tuvalu Islands or Three Mile Island, or New Orleans or the Ukraine, or, or, or.

Although it is becoming harder and harder to believe that the "really bad environmental problems" are somewhere "over there," somehow we compartmentalize our lives. We have families; we go to church or synagogue. We recycle. We live our lives and hope that Government or Technology or the Free Market will fix it all.

That's where I was in 1988 on the third day after my youngest daughter was born. I was lying in bed with the rush of feeling that women can have during that amazing passage. My body was flush with those hormones that give the tribe of women the power to protect their young.

On this particular summer day, my hazy maternal reverie was pierced by an announcement on the radio that this was a "Bad Air Quality Day." I heard the news over the hum of the freeway traffic just outside my window in my cozy New England suburb. Bad Air Quality Day. What did the governor say? What does that mean? Is there a ban on driving nonemergency vehicles? Do we hold our breath until the next weather front passes through? Why doesn't anybody seem to think that this is an *emergency*? Finally, a word from our governor: "If you are asthmatic or elderly, don't exercise outside." Well, that cuts to the root of the problem, doesn't it?

The terrible contradiction had broken through into my bones. We are full of life … and we are poisoning ourselves. I laid there for a long time considering the matter. I had lain down on that bed a mother. And I stood up a Matriot. I could see that the way to care for my young was *not* to ignore the consequences of our actions but to gently, lovingly nudge us all toward a sustainable future.

That day I wrote a two-page document and called it "Many Small Steps." I spelled out simple, practical actions that I envisioned as ways to build community and control waste. Writing down these steps galvanized my activism and forced me to think through my daily actions and the impact on the environment. I envision advocacy as a series of "small steps" all of us can take. Here are a few things I included (see the Appendices in the back of the book for the complete list):

Many Small Steps

We are a network of individuals who are committed to making the changes—large and small—in our lifestyles that will allow us to live in a compatible way with the resources of our planet.

There are no dues; there is no age limitation for membership. To become a member you must choose at least three "Small Steps" from this list to begin doing immediately. Add at least one step each week until you are living the most ecological lifestyle you can. You cannot join on behalf of anyone else. Each of us must make our own commitment.

- I will avoid buying/using clothing that requires dry cleaning.

- I will choose food and other products in the most ecological packaging available (paper, cotton, and glass, as opposed to plastic).

- I will start/expand my garden.

- I will stop using toxic sprays on my lawn.

- I will establish a bartering relationship with a neighbor (child care for knitting lessons?).

- I will set a radius (two blocks? two miles?) and make a commitment to walk everywhere I need to go within that radius.

- I will donate or find a use for items I no longer wish to use.

- I will make a sustained effort to turn off appliances and lights that are not in use.

- I will use my/our children's "artwork" as stationery when writing to relatives.

- I will eat the most wholesome and unadulterated diet possible.

- I will support businesses that promote environmental awareness.

- I will ask my grocer to carry local/organic produce.

- I will ask my grocer to carry alternatives to Styrofoam products.

- I will enjoy moments outside each day.

- I will learn about the vegetation and wildlife in my area.

TOO GOOD TO BE TRUE!

I started with small, doable, positive steps because that's what we each have control over. The local copy shop ran off "Many Small Steps" for me—on recycled paper—and my career as an activist shifted into high gear.

I started with the power of the shopping cart. I didn't have the patience for legislative processes. Lobbyists from the plastics industries had many more men in suits than I had babysitters. They could show up at every hearing, and I could barely keep track of the postponed ones. Lobbyists spent the days between canceled hearings in restaurants and hotel rooms; I spent those days in the laundry room. But I persisted. I became a homemaker activist; I led from the nursery.

In the early eighties, recycling was not the institution it is today. Fledgling "demonstration" projects were set up here and there, but most people considered their garbage to be garbage, not *materials*. The local paper covered me because—astonishingly—I set aside a small area in the mudroom to keep reusable stuff so I could sort and distribute it appropriately. I wonder whether this radical act of sedition earned me an FBI file.

Lobbyists for the American Plastics Industry were in town because our state was considering a mandatory recycling bill. The industry sent their delegates to Hartford, where I live, because they were against the idea. I, meanwhile, spent my days calling all the recyclers in the state to find out who would voluntarily take the stuff from my mud porch. Yet, while the plastics' lobbyists were endorsing voluntary recycling, I found not a single site in the state that would take my plastics.

That night on the news, I happened to see a commercial sponsored by Dow Chemical Company. In the commercial, a group of healthy and sympathetic hikers were dismayed to find a discarded plastic plate on the trail. Frowns all around! One hiker brightly chirped, "Plastics are recyclable!"

"Plastics are recyclable?!" the others inquired. This was too good to be true!

"Yes," replied Hiker Number 1. "Plastics are recyclable!"

Never mind that someone in the group would have to volunteer to take the plate home with them and call all the recyclers in their home state to see what, exactly, they should do with the plate. We were all just supposed to feel reassured by the knowledge that Plastics Are Recyclable. Problem solved.

I was stunned. How much does it cost to buy airtime on the nightly news? Was it possible that the plastics industry was as avid about solving this problem as I was?

I got on the phone and tracked down a corporate office for Dow Chemical Company. As luck would have it, my first choice of New Jersey yielded a result. I had a name and an address. Thus armed, I gathered all my cheese wrappers and yogurt containers and milk cartons and damaged rubber duckies into three large boxes and shipped them off to New Jersey. In the cover letter I explained that I was a humble activist-homemaker, and it never would have occurred to me to educate the public that Plastics Are Recyclable on the evening news. I was ever so grateful that Dow had the financial resources and the will to do such effective activism. Unfortunately, I continued, no one in my state would accept these wastes. Strangely, plastic industry representatives were currently fighting mandatory recycling in my state. That is a bit confusing, isn't it? But in any event, now that I had this gentleman's address, I could forward my recyclables to him directly. I was sure he would know just what to do with them.

If you have ever done this kind of consumer activism, you are aware that I received a very polite letter that began, "Dear Ms. Cohen-Kiener: Thank you for your interest in plastics recycling ..." I was informed that my valuable resources had been shipped off to the demonstration plastic recycling site in Ohio. A young man named Doug was in charge of the company's efforts there, and he would be happy to handle my materials.

Of course I called Doug. "Hello, Doug? This is Andrea ..." Thus began one of the more uncomfortable conversations of Doug's career. Doug really was an environmentalist, living in the heart of the beast. He was actually *the* environmentalist in the whole plastics industry. This position gave him some small hope of changing things from the inside. I asked him a number of rather pointed questions about his demonstration project. Is it viable, for example? It turns out that the plastic materials he was collecting from neighborhoods in Ohio were reshaped into flowerpots and combs that each had a street value of $0.79 cents but cost around $38 to make. Not too promising for a transition to a free market. I asked whether Doug's work would be helped or hindered by mandatory recycling ordinances. "Helped," he admitted. Then why, I wondered out loud, would his employer's trade association be fighting our efforts in Hartford? Doug had no good answer for this. We spent time talking about which types of plastic polymers had any promise of true recyclability, what could be done to simplify the waste stream, barriers to recycling, what *precycling* could look like, and so on. Doug helped me frame some constructive questions that I could share with my legislators, and we—the recycling people—did win that fight in Connecticut. A sliver of the plastic waste in our state was incorporated into the recycling stream.

We have a long way to go to simplify the waste stream, to reduce the amount of trash we generate, and to recapture much more of the waste stream. Eighteen years after that battle, a scant 6 percent of plastic materials are recycled nationwide.

THE SPIRITUAL CHALLENGE
OF A MOUNTAIN OF GARBAGE

The spiritual challenge of a mountain of garbage may not be readily evident.

I learned that there is a spiritual component to the mountain of garbage from my neighbor Jack. After the birth of my daughter, I was in the front yard enjoying a sunny day when I saw that Neighbor Jack was throwing out some bottles. At the time, I was participating in voluntary recycling, which meant that I saved my reusable stuff and, when the pile threatened to take over the mudroom and spill into the kitchen, I carted it down to the town dump. And here was Neighbor Jack carelessly throwing his bottles away! I was sad. I was angry. I was afraid. Jack's wanton acts of waste were endangering *my* planet, *my* babies. Why, I had a good mind to march right over there and … and what? Shame him? Rage at him? Jack was not an evil or destructive man. I was shocked at how destructive my rage felt. I realized that there was very little I could repair by marching over to Jack's house in this condition. What if I offered to take Jack's bottles with me next time I went to the dump? That would build community *and* reduce waste. That would be an act of caring for creation and loving my neighbor as myself. This was the moment I first knew that there is a spiritual component to the very concrete environmental challenges we face.

I began to pay attention to my motives and my emotional states as I engaged in environmental activism. Usually, my actions were rooted in fear and anger. I was afraid that we were despoiling the planet. I was afraid that we were making ourselves sick. I was angry that people were just too lazy, greedy, or numbed out to care. But why would anyone want to join me in the revolution if it required being angry and afraid all the time? And, anyway, could I really clean up the environment on the physical plane if I was mucking it up on the emotional level? I needed to rethink my approach to the trash mountain.

I started with the basics: Where does the trash mountain come from? It comes from all of us doing all the normal things we do: growing out of clothes, buying canned peas, decorating our homes. All the day-to-day things we do to feed and comfort our bodies create waste. Is it wrong to want a lovely home? Contrary to what Mom always said, is it wrong to eat our peas?

No. But it is wrong, in a way, to be unconscious and discon-nected. It is good for us, as evolving human-spiritual beings, to be aware of where our peas come from (and our curtains and our shoes, and so forth). It is good for us, and for the environment, to be aware of where these materials go when we are done with them. We are—each of us—a small part of something grand and amazing. When we feel that connection, we are naturally motivated not to despoil the planet that is the source of all our blessings.

This sense of connection, this feeling of being "part of," this awareness of the preciousness of life—for me, this is the crux of spiritual values and the core of environmental activism.

We are in a relationship with the trash mountain. We are its creators. We are in a relationship with Indonesian sweatshops and burning Amazon forest lands. Our appetites fuel these things. We are in a relationship with nitrogen runoff into the Chesapeake Bay and carbon emissions emanating from the caravan of eighteen-wheelers that whiz across our nation daily. It is how we gain our daily bread that requires and supports these things. We are precipitating a change in the very climate, land, and water that sustain us.

We are connected to all of this. When we are unconscious of it, we are less aware of who and what we are. When we are disconnected from it, we have no motive to behave differently. The double-edged sword of the preciousness of life is this: We are a tiny part of the whole of the cosmos, and we are a tiny part of these destructive systems.

As a human being, I am concerned about what these messes mean for my health and our children's future. As a religious person, I am concerned about what it all means about our state of awareness, our spirit, and our faithfulness to our purpose. Can we be responsible cocreators with God when we despoil and destroy the very life-sustaining capacity of earth? The sicknesses in our bodies—the asthmas and cancers—are calling our attention. The physical problems point us to the spiritual misalignment.

AGENTS FOR TRANSFORMATION

In the early years of modern environmentalism, it seemed as if we could win our battles by signing petitions or by cleaning up the beach on a Sunday. We could pass a local ordinance and that would suffice to get recycling going or close a landfill.

Global warming is different.

Climate change is pervasive and global. It is well under way. It is not going to respond to local measures alone. Climate change is just the issue that is big enough to prove to us—once and for all—that we are connected. It is a big enough challenge to finally focus our minds on the common good.

We are in the midst of a global brush with mortality. As individuals, we know what it is like to live with a brush with mortality. Many of you reading this book have had your near misses or are living with a chronic, possibly fatal, disease, as I am living with cancer. We have gone through the stages of grief, from denial to acceptance. I count it as a special blessing that I know my days are numbered. I cannot ignore this, as many can, as I could have before cancer. My time is precious. In the face of the possibility of losing everything, I made serious recalculations about what was important, what was enduring, what was uniquely possible for me. Every day I live since the cancer diagnosis is a fuller day, a day that I am closer to my essence. I have more joy and satisfaction now, in the face of my mortality, than I did in my blissful ignorance.

Individuals who have had a brush with mortality can, and do, find ways to wake up each day, to find purpose and spirit. Knowing our finitude gives us the courage to say no to the superfluous.

Humanity is facing a collective brush with mortality, yet we are still in the stage of denial. There are hundreds of thousands of global warming deaths already, deaths that are not tallied this way on the news. A professor I knew fell through the ice at his family cottage in the woods in deep Maine—in January, a time when the ice was usually thick enough to support him. A child from Connecticut died in a park when a tree branch, weakened by pests and mold, fell off the tree and landed on his head. Some of the intense fighting in Darfur is about water scarcity, which is exacerbating hunger. A percentage of the death toll from Katrina and other intensified weather phenomena are due to climate change. Tens of thousands have died across Europe and the United States of stultifying heat waves in the early years of this century alone. The news media report these stories as isolated tragedies. They are not. They are symptoms of one disease—climate change.

Global warming may sound nice, like a Florida vacation, but its consequences are devastating. The die-off of forest stands and bats and bees are ominous harbingers of things to come. What will we eat when food crops are not pollinated by bees? What will we eat when the breadbasket regions of the world are beset by turbulent weather, floods, and droughts? Climate change, global scorching (a phrase used by Rabbi Arthur Waskow to generate the proper level of concern), and weather aberrations are already upon us.

One of the blessings in Deuteronomy is the promise of normal weather in the proper season. And the curse is the opposite. Unpredictable weather, not in the due season, results in the human community "quickly disappearing from the good land that God gives you" (Deuteronomy 11:17).

It is urgent and necessary that we wake up to the danger facing us, yet it is overwhelming and frightening to do so. In order to be awake, we must travel the five stages of grief (denial, anger, bargaining, depression, and acceptance) again and again, and bring others with us. It is emotionally difficult work—work that requires self-awareness and strength and gentleness.

We can hear the voices of these five stages of grief on the radio and in our conversations with our friends:

Denial: It's not happening. It's not that bad. It's not caused by humans.

Anger: Pointy-headed liberals are trying to control us. If they have their way, we'll all be living in caves. If we have to wear sweaters and turn down our thermostat, the terrorists will have won.

Bargaining: Let's let the market take care of it. Maybe we can cap and trade carbon emissions.

Depression: It's too late to do anything about it. We're doomed.

Acceptance: What is in my power to affect and influence, to put us on a more sustainable course? I will take action and encourage others to act as well—to reverse the deleterious consequences of our current lifestyle.

If we wake up and work together, addressing the deep roots of the problem, we may be able to ameliorate the consequences of global warming and adapt. If we begin to contemplate the life cycles of the objects we buy and use—not just recycling, but precycling: Where does our stuff come from? Where is it going?—we will be more conscious of the environmental impact that our consumption has. And we will wake up to our relationship with a whole host of environmental problems. We will begin to feel an agitation that is true and useful. This agitation is the call of spirit, asking us to appreciate more and use less. This awareness is the power we need to be agents for transformation.

We will need to work for many years until we see any abatement, and the harm already done will affect us for centuries. *We will have to have faith* that we are doing the right thing by working together to reduce the causes of global climate change. And we will have to find the joy and the blessing as we go along.

THE ULTIMATE COMMON GROUND

The environmental challenge is an issue that respects no class and national boundary. The impacts of global climate change affect the rich (who generate most of the carbon emissions) and subsistence farmers around the world (who generate none of it) alike. The wives of ExxonMobil executives die of breast cancer, and the children of Monsanto employees suffer from childhood leukemia, just like the rest of us. Wall Street executives living on the Connecticut Gold Coast suffer from asthma just as urban African-American kids and Chinese citizens do. The air and the seas and the soil of this planet are our common heritage. The earth is the ultimate common ground.

In the movie *Independence Day*, humans rally together to defend their common sphere against a common enemy—an alien invasion. Our situation is similar. We are well on the way to altering the global conditions that support life as we know it. Shifts in weather conditions have already created a new category of displaced persons: environmental refugees. Migration of species are so well under way that all of us with eyes to see have observed, in the span of a lifetime, the die-off of stands of familiar trees and the migration of new plants, shellfish, bugs, and mammals. The world outside our windows is changing as Mother Nature adapts in her wisdom to the changing conditions we create. Life on earth will go on, and there is no *need* for us to save the planet. We may, on the other hand, wish to create conditions that will further the human project on earth. We may wish to act—to save ourselves.

2

The Makings of a Movement

The Interfaith Imperative and Its Obstacles

THE MOUNTAIN OF GOD

THERE IS A PARABLE ABOUT A MOUNTAIN. The mountain leads to God, but it's rather large and it looks like a hard climb. From the boot camp at the base of the mountain, I can only see my people, and of course, I assume that only my people are graced or intelligent enough to know where the path up the mountain is. So I begin my climb. Some of my own people aren't brave enough even to do that, but something in me propels me onward … I have to find out. I climb. It's hard. It's very hard to climb. I'm out of shape, which I did not realize until I began this effort. And the backpack that I carry, full of tradition and rituals—my God, it is heavy! I am sore. It is dark on this climb and it is lonely. I am often afraid, and there is little in the way of reward. But, to tell the truth, I have my arrogance to comfort me; it is my small reward for my labors. "At least I am doing this! Others never even got started!"

How much time goes by? I climb and climb. I am stronger now. It is actually exhilarating to climb. I never knew I could feel this power. My backpack is a breeze to me; it is an aid to my balance. The tree cover begins to break now. I can see that others have been here before me at this level. I can see that there are other paths that begin at other base camps and that climbers can climb this high on all those paths as well. I hadn't been able to see this until I reached this point. I am well above the tree line now, and I see that the mountain is very small compared to the vastness to which it points. It's all God from here on up, and all my tools, all my words are inadequate. At the peak of my ascent, I am most humbled. I am most curious—compelled by a sense of urgency— to know of the ways of the other climbers. Surely it is a glory to God to search for this.

OBSTACLES ON THE PATH

I started with this parable about diversity because there are some craggy mountain paths to climb on the way to our interfaith coalition to save the environment. There are many obstacles along the way that we need to both acknowledge and address.

Different Languages

The question of language is central. Each religious tradition has its own vocabulary and symbols for its values. If we are willing to see these vocabulary words as ideas that can be translated, we can find shared meaning and common ground with people who do not share our native "language."

A Christian, for example, might see Jesus, in addition to many other things, as a symbol for the promise of renewal after moments of desolation. But desolation and renewal are universal and natural. Day follows night, and the Qur'an teaches that the phenomena of darkness and light in nature are a sign for people who pay attention, a sign of what is true in every life. From God's first contact with Father Abraham in Genesis, we are guaranteed rising and falling fortunes. Embedded in the very first letter of the Bible, the Hebrew *bet* (signifying two), is understood by Jewish sages to mean that we live in a world of dichotomy, of blessings and curses.

A psychological, lived resurrection can be true and meaningful for people of all faiths.

Different Questions

Besides language, there is the question of questions. In essence, each major religion is interested in significantly different questions. Religious communities have divergent theologies, philosophies, and sociologies, and even when these systems have important values in common, the overlapping concern isn't always obvious because they don't ask the same core questions. Christianity, for example, seems to give precedence to questions of personal salvation. And Judaism, while interested in faithful connections to God, is more devoted overall to making sense out of the collective history of the Jewish people in relation to God and the nations of the world.

Sometimes burning questions are foisted upon us by historical conditions. Islam today, for example, is living a dispersion that has brought large Muslim populations to new corners of the world, unrivaled since the time of the Muslim conquests of the early Middle Ages. Many Muslim communities today—of necessity—are preoccupied with questions of continuity and adaptation to the new conditions. How can Muslims be faithful, responsible, and responsive in Detroit and London?

There will also be times when we do not see eye to eye on every component of the ecological crisis. Overpopulation is a key example. The sheer number of us *is* an issue. Some think that it is *the* issue. These advocates urge any means of limiting population growth. The Catholic community and others, however, cannot include population abatement in their environmental work. It is the Catholic "culture of life" that informs their creation care ethic; controlling population growth cannot be part of it. The first commandment, after all, is to "be fruitful and multiply."

We will not change each other's minds or behavior on this issue. When this question comes up in our work together, I recommend that we not tear the dialogue apart; we do not need to get stuck on this point. We can work together at the consumption side of the equation. In the United States, 4 percent of the population consumes 25 percent of earth's resources! There is much we can work on together without getting divided by different questions.

Historical Wounds

There are also historical wounds between us, deep-seated animosities that have festered through generations, even centuries, and create seemingly insurmountable barriers to communication and understanding. Deep theological divisions separate Christians, Jews, and Muslims. Historical wounds are embedded in our recent histories. It is easy, perhaps natural, for us to feel suspicious of each other, wary. This is also true within denominations.

Members of a minority group or a group that sees itself as the victim of discrimination will be less self-reflective in an interfaith forum. Black or Jewish Americans might claim prejudicial injustice as a unique structure by which we have been particularly disadvantaged, rather than a condition of the human mind. We might experience our historical grievances as grounds for self-preservation, not grounds for universalism.

The Need to Be "Right"

In essence, faith groups are in competition with each other for the souls (and the membership dues!) of the believer. And the more imperiled members of a particular faith group feel, the less interested they are in playing nicely with the other denominations. Indeed, it takes a very secure person to actually be interested in seeing their religious experience and language in comparison with another. Many of our platitudes about all believing in one God are so vague as to be almost meaningless. We are often afraid to discuss head-on any points of disagreement. Most of us experience our faith as our way of being right with God and humanity, not as religious and psychological phenomena. Our idea that we are the Right Ones is deeply challenged when we begin to see that there may be many good paths. We may lose our sense of uniqueness, of being God's chosen or special ones.

The obstacles to interfaith coalition are very real, but we also face the very real challenge of preserving creation. It is imperative that we try! As people of faith, we make up 70 percent of the population and, collectively, we have the mandate, power, and credibility to put eco-justice into motion. As individuals and as faith communions, we have unique capacities and a unique role. We are alive in the context of the web of life. We must sustain it or we risk the future of humanity itself.

Just as in the natural world, our diversity is a treasure, not a plague. If we look at species of bugs and plants, life flourishes in unique cracks and crannies, from the desert dune to the deep, deep sea. God, it seems, treasures diversity more than we do. Can we muster the deep respect, indeed the deep, interdependent *need,* for all these boisterous, holy paths up the mountain of God?

We need to speak about our shared truths. If we are aware of our shared values shining through our particular language, we can find more common ground with more folks. This becomes possible when we are able to climb out of our base camp and come closer to the top of the mountain of God.

GOD OF THE PEWS OR GOD OF THE COSMOS?

In the base camp of our traditions, we have picked our little corner of the religious world to make a home and to practice in. From that vantage point, we cannot see that there is anyone else facing the huge project of the climb. Yet as environmental devastation becomes more obvious, and as we begin to understand how many of our problems are interconnected with ecological issues, we may find ourselves ready to seek the voice in each of our traditions that will speak to these concerns. We may be motivated to hear from each other.

Interfaith work and the call to environmental work tugs at the same folks. These are the folks who are looking for commonalities. I am the director of an interfaith environmental organization in Connecticut called Interreligious Eco-Justice Network (IREJN). The founders were inspired by an Episcopal priest named Sally "Eco-Sal" Bingham. At the time, Sally was leading a group called Episcopal Power and Light (EPL) as a religious response to global warming. Sally soon went through a political reality check and quickly transformed EPL into IPL, Interfaith Power and Light. IPL now has offices in twenty-nine states. In these states, denominations that don't always "play nicely together" are now working together just fine.

In some cases, the environmental partnerships are more like parallel play. Some of our colleagues in Connecticut and other states feel that they will be more effective if they reach out to their own faith groups. If a Catholic speaks to a Catholic, or a Jew to a Jew, or a Muslim to a Muslim, or an evangelical to an evangelical, the environmental message might pass the "smell test" more readily.

A few years ago an Episcopal priest called IREJN and asked for a speaker on faith-based activism and climate change. She requested an Episcopalian speaker, but it was a little harder for me to get a Christian from our speakers' list to give a talk on a Sunday because that is their day with their home congregation. As I rabbi, I am free on Sunday mornings, and I love to visit these houses of worship, so I offered my services. "But if you come," the priest said, strategically, "the topic will be 'The Issue of the Week.' If an Episcopalian comes, our members will see this issue as part of all the other things we are building together."

This priest's comments are highly instructive. Every individual and every community has a natural, rightful self-interest. For some denominations and for some individuals and congregations, it is crucial to see this issue within the frame of their own faith lens. As an interfaith organizer, my job at that moment was to get that congregation a speaker who spoke their language.

For others, something quite different is true. Universalists and some individual congregations, typically those comprising liberal Christians and Jews, seem to feel that the message is more powerful if it comes from an outside messenger. Part of the hope they feel when it comes to stewardship of the planet stems from the numbers and the kinds of people who are engaged in it.

Yet the idea of shared values and shared action with other faith traditions can be threatening to our insularity. It might be okay for poetic speeches, but finding common cause on the environment might just be the camel's nose poking into the tent that will disrupt our denominational certitude. There are very few interfaith settings that are safe enough for the participants to get past the platitudes. To speak truthfully about the limitations of our coreligionists or the disappointment they cause us to feel might seem disloyal in an interfaith setting. And to say publicly what we really think about the faith traditions we haven't chosen—how could we do that without being rude? And then there's the whole liberal label to contend with. Earth care smells a little secular to some because it's the scientists and environmentalists who started it all!

As a rabbi, I am called by the Jewish tradition to perpetuate a particular religious tradition. Creation care pulls me in the opposite direction. The mandate to stewardship calls me to work with many others. Those others may disagree with me about a just solution in Israel/Palestine. Those others may disagree with me about the divinity of Jesus or the journey of the soul after death. They might disagree with each other about these and many other issues. But we cannot get the job of environmental repair done if we stay hunkered down in our base camps. We must work together.

Faith-based environmental work is not one-size-fits-all, and it is not a green pastiche over what already exists. This movement asks people to bring their own faith to bear on urgent human and theological issues. Is the God of the pews of this congregation the God of the cosmos? If so, what is our proper relationship to earth and the other faith communities?

The environmental crisis challenges us to love the God of creation more than the God of the pews. Our dogma will not help us here; our experience of the living universe will. And it is just this experience of the living universe that we sometimes resist and fear because it pulls us out of the comfort zone of our particular beliefs or practices.

LEAVING BASE CAMP

The movement out of the base camp is evolutionary. We leave that safe haven when a discomfort that cannot be alleviated forces us to do so. We could stay there all our lives; many do. But some of us feel a dissatisfaction there. We sense that our way may not be the only way. Some other truth or expression has become known to us that cannot be accounted for in the language of the base camp. We move out and confront the unknown because the discomfort within becomes too great, greater than our resistance to leaving.

There are four key steps we can take to begin the climb out of our base camp.

Reclaim the Green Roots in Our Own Traditions

When we truly are called to earth care, there is usually a realignment of the relationship with our faith of origin. We begin to understand that the God of the cosmos is so much larger than the God of our creeds. Sometimes this realignment is difficult. We may have read the Psalms about the hills dancing and the trees clapping as poetry, but not imagined ourselves praying along with all creation. We may have read of the simple daily bread of the founders and fathers and prophets of our traditions as quaint and distant customs, not as a mandate to satisfy our needs simply, rather than overindulging. We may even be reading our texts through our modern eyes, yet very few of us have "green" eyes. Ironically, the first steps out of base camp usually result in a deep reclamation of the dark-green roots of our very own tradition.

When I began to look at my faith through green eyes, I found many traditions that would be considered deeply environmental by today's standards. An ethic of balanced consumption, appreciation, and the general mandate to tend the garden permeates the Jewish tradition. For example, although there is no law that tells us we must vote "no" on new construction projects, Jews are told, by the Talmud, not to live in a town with no greenery. There is no rule for preservation of open spaces, but according to the Torah, even in war, we cannot cut down fruit trees nor salt the soil. These techniques were used by ancient warriors to make land unsuitable for agriculture, to starve the enemy.

We are commanded in Torah to "bury our waste" outside the camp and told that a spade for this purpose is among the tools of war. It is astonishing to me that waste composting is required even in the destructive rush of war. How would Torah guide us with respect to bottle redemption and curbside recycling?

Up to 70 percent of processed food in the American market contains products of genetic engineering, including soft drinks, catsup, potato chips, cookies, ice cream, and cornflakes, according to a CBS news report in 2001. Lubavitch Rabbi Yossi Serebryanski, a kosher supervisor, said he has stopped eating tomatoes and only eats potatoes he knows are organic. He fears that genes from non-kosher foods, such as pigs or insects, could be implanted in vegetables and Jews may unwittingly break kosher laws by eating them, according to *The Curmudgeon Cow*, in February 2009.

Traditional Jews are not allowed to interbreed species of animals or seed stock. How would Torah guide us on genetic alterations that put flounder DNA into tomatoes?

29

On the other hand, the Jewish tradition is friendly to science and research. Humans are seen as cocreators of the universe, and our imagination is one of the gifts we possess as creatures in the divine image. We live with a tension between innovation and hubris, between natural laws and the needs of human industry.

Our holidays are seasonal and cyclical. Every Sabbath, I am aware of the time of the setting sun because earth time, not clock time, is the standard for the start and end of Sabbath. This point is so subtly powerful. Almost nothing in Western culture pulls us to earth time. With the advent of indoor lighting, heating systems, snowplows, and the like, we are impervious to, and cut off from, the seasons. We tell time in our culture by the commercial calendar more than the natural calendar. White sales follow Christmas specials. Valentine's chocolates and jewelry follow that, then the corned beef and cabbage of St. Patrick's Day, and so on. But my holiday calendar calls me to the Festival of Lights during the winter solstice. The three major festivals of Passover, Shavuot, and Sukkot are all rooted in the farming cycles of planting and harvest.

When I study tradition, I become aware of how much we have lost our natural heritage and, with it, a vital connection. We are poorer for it and mostly unaware of the majesty we are missing. Indoors, it takes a conscious effort for us to remember that we are a small speck in the cosmos. For Abraham, Moses, Jesus, and Muhammad in the wilderness, the remembrance was all around them. Our founders were teaching us about proper consumption as well as proper belief. It will require new eyes to see these teachings in our texts and to embody them in our lives.

Find a Common Language

In base camp, adherents may speak about receiving the Holy Spirit or Grace or Shechinah (God's energizing nearness in the Jewish tradition) or Revelation or Dharma (wisdom in the Buddhist way). All these are specific articulations of our need to sense divine presence, to interact with the living universe. In an interfaith setting we can continue to find power in these ideas, but we can also meet each other in our smallness, in our ever-present need, in our shared human condition. We can speak of gratitude, appreciation, and understanding, which are all true ways to describe our interdependence.

The very challenge of environmental effort requires all our faiths, our actions, and our commitment. We need all the spiritual tools of prayer, centering, and meditation to counter despair; to support our faithful action; to nourish us and keep the work delightful. This presents a new challenge for those of us who have made it to the interfaith table. What is the language for our gatherings?

I am often the (sole) rabbi at various interfaith events, and I am often brought up short at the moment of opening prayers or closing prayers that are so clearly, if unconsciously, Christological. I am reminded of why Jewish people, and other non-Christians, might avoid so-called "interfaith" events. Over the years, I have practiced the art of translating the prayers that I hear at these events into words that I believe, words that I can say "Amen" to. To simply not pray at these meetings is one option. But that seems contrary to who we are and why we are motivated to be at the interfaith environmental-action meeting in the first place. There is energy available when we name the Oneness on whose behalf we work that is a kind of fuel for our gatherings.

At one such event, a priest was asked to say a prayer before the meal. He spoke very beautifully, and I could hear him beginning to close his blessing with a phrase that was going to end with "… in the Name of the Father and the Son and the Holy Ghost." I felt myself pull back ever so slightly. I had been so caught up in the moment, and now I was going to need to engage my inner translator. My colleague also sensed what was happening, and he paused ever so briefly, ending his prayer with "in Your Name."

Such a small step for him, and yet he gave up something to do it, perhaps something more than a habitual phrase. Perhaps he was sacrificing the power of some very specific imagery that held particular meaning for him. But something was gained as well: a wider partnership, more *Amens*, more blessings, more hearts in praise together—not a small thing!

What I find when I seek ways to speak about the God of the cosmos in an interfaith setting is that, by coming home to the universals within my faith tradition, my language is naturally more inclusive. I say *cosmos* more than *heaven*—a word that is laden with particularist understandings. *Cosmos* allows me to include scientists and nontheists, and I can speak about the complexity of creation, the powerful order and intelligence and dance of existence.

In an interfaith setting, I also refer to *light, season,* and *nature*—all real and shared phenomena. The earth is shared with other people, even the secular, even the scientists. These natural phenomena are shared with other creatures and life-forms. When I use these words, I am reminded of the centrality of this message within my tradition. I hear anew the words of Psalms about the hills rejoicing and the stars praising. I hear a deeper intent in the specific Jewish liturgical poems that shape the morning prayer and the evening prayer. Again and again, I find that the more I am true to my own tradition, the deeper the connection I have with others in interfaith settings. And the more I engage in faith conversation and work with non-Jews, the more all-encompassing my Judaism becomes.

I find that my colleagues in interfaith environmental work have a similar experience. Their own religious perspective is wider and deeper when their God is named in many ways. Not only do they sense that religious folks can save the environment, but they also recognize that the environmental challenge can reinvigorate religious traditions in meaningful and important ways.

Get Beyond the Need to Be Right

When we begin to expand our language, we may begin to wonder whether we can stay loyal to the fold and to the new experience at the same time. We may have a sense that our doctrinal language is too small to speak adequately about the felt truth of our aliveness in the cosmos. Yet because our words don't seem particularly Jewish or Baptist, we may feel uneasy, on unfamiliar ground.

Catholic, African-American, Hispanic, and Muslim allies have told me that when they speak about the call to advance stewardship of the planet, they feel that their loyalty to the pressing issues of their "group" is called into question. An Episcopal friend told me that when she described her newfound experience of the living God, she was labeled an "Episco-pagan." Mathew Sleeth, a prominent evangelical proponent of creation care, said that when he felt God in the living world, it was like his conversion to Christ—no small metaphor for an evangelical! The God of special connection with the Christian flock is also the God of the stars and the microbes, and even the unsaved.

A conservative religious ally, Dr. Lowell "Rusty" Pritchard, urges us beyond our black/white, conservative/liberal labels: "Conservatism is scared of change. I ask people, 'What is it that conservatives should be conserving?' We need to conserve all that makes human civilization good and beautiful and diverse. We can respect diversity because it's a blessing from God. That takes us past the shallow conservatism of fearing new ideas and deeper to a conservatism that says we ought to do our best to take care of the natural world."

We flirt with arrogance when we cling to a guiding philosophy. Yet we are more apt to notice that arrogance in others who hold obstinately to *their* truths, while we, on the other hand, have *the* truth. This arrogance is as distasteful on the Right as it is on the Left. Are we in this together or not? And here is the key question: Do we want to be right or do we want to be effective?

Many of us equate our religious identity with the experience of being okay or right, or the Right Ones. This subtle self-satisfaction, if left unexamined, is the root of xenophobia and religious triumphalism. And this self-satisfaction is not the pitfall of one faith tradition or another; it is in the nature of our desire to be religious, to be pious, to be close to God. The hard face of self-righteousness can be found in every faith tradition.

However, if we want to be effective in saving our beautiful planet, we need to put aside our hard-earned *isms*. We need to translate our values into frames that others can share. We need to ask open-ended questions and listen for common concerns in the answers. We need to admit that we do not know all the answers, but insist that we have urgent questions to consider.

John Grim, cofounder of the Harvard Forum on Religion and Ecology, convenes leadership from all of the world's religions to explore and enhance environmental stewardship. He tells a story that I call the "last day of the conference." He says the first days of the gatherings are full of elevated teachings and poetic platitudes about how our texts and role models call us to be stewards of the earth. Sometime late in the conference, one brave soul says something more grounded, such as "I'm not sure we are living up to this teaching in my tradition" or "Other concerns seem to take precedence over earth stewardship." This reality check usually initiates an outpouring of humility and concern, and the conference begins in earnest, minutes before it ends.

It is much more useful for us to be aware and accurate than it is for us to impress each other with the wisdom of our tradition. The wisdom of our tradition will speak for itself, if we are living it. The challenge is to stop defending our dogmas and bolstering our self-satisfaction and start examining our lived environmental stewardship. We are all in this together.

Forge New Partnerships

When we find ourselves climbing higher up the mountain, we will see that we are not alone; we have never been alone. There are others on the climb. Some started in our base camp and others did not. These are our compatriots, these are our new partners.

Reaching beyond our comfort zone to work with people of other faiths takes a little courage and a lot of openness. We need to be able to explore without preconceptions, listen without prejudgment, and dialogue without preconditions. But what we can learn from each other, and what we can accomplish together, is very much worth the effort!

I am particularly enthusiastic about forging partnerships with American mosques. Islam is the fastest-growing religious group in the United States, but many Jewish and Christian congregations are fearful or skeptical of crossing the divide. Recently, I had a conversation with Mohamad A. Chakaki, a Muslim environmental activist and community organizer who is active in the Greater Washington Power and Light. Mohamad alerted me to the fact that Islam, in and of itself, is enormously, perhaps uniquely, diverse as a faith community. There are Muslims of every race, many nationalities, and varied income levels in the American Muslim community. Some African-American Muslims were brought here centuries ago from Africa; some black Muslims converted in the sixties and seventies in the context of other expressions of black solidarity and organizing. Muslims who are immigrants (many first or second generation) may want very much to blend in to their new milieu, and others hold strong ties of identity to Indonesia, Palestine, Iran, and the many other countries from which they migrated. Like it or not, Muslims find themselves caught up in the embedded political conflict between the United States and Muslim countries. It is a challenging time to be a Muslim in America.

I see two particular benefits this diverse community brings to the environmental movement. First, Islamic philosophy is exquisitely sensitive to the important interplay among humans, the earth, and the divine. In the Qur'an, there is a seamless web, an expression of God that is alive in our inner environment as well as our cosmic home. Mohamad A. Chakaki told me that he is a student of architecture, among other interests, partly because he believes that our built environment can reflect and enhance our living connection to God. Our building materials and designs can also have the opposite impact of distancing us from the divine and distorting our very spirits. The philosophy of Islam offers us beautiful language and insight as faith-based earth stewards.

The second reason I believe that our movement will be strengthened by Muslim participation is the very fact of the social diversity within the American Islamic community. Muslim Americans who are nonwhite are going to make our movement even more sensitive to environmental health and justice issues. Muslims who are newer to the United States are going to help us become ever more aware of the global impact of climate change, pollution, deforestation, and all the rest.

In my many conversations with Muslim allies, Baptists, evangelicals and others, we are frequently astonished and pleased that we have found so much shared passion. We see in our own hearts and in our coalitions that it is possible to create partnerships wide and powerful enough to confront the intertwined issues before us. These partnerships—this caring and this trust—we must earn from each other.

THE ONE ABOUT THE RABBI AND THE EVANGELICAL

Even in my zeal for diversity, I did not imagine that I could find much common cause with evangelicals. As a nice Jewish girl growing up in the suburbs of Billy Graham country, my sole association with evangelicals was as folks who thought I would eventually be going to hell.

But there I was at a conference at Yale, and I noticed this fellow across the room who just emanated kindness. I made an effort to find out more about this gentleman and realized that he was Dr. Lowell "Rusty" Pritchard, officially the national outreach director for the Evangelical Environmental Network and editor of *Creation Care* magazine. He is one of a large and growing cadre of conservative Christians who find that earth care is part and parcel of their faith commitment.

I had the opportunity to have a dialogue with Rusty, under the auspices of the magazine *Sh'ma: A Journal of Jewish Responsibility.* I was curious about how Rusty would root creation care in the First and Second Testaments. He told me that he looks to Genesis to teach about care of creation, but more often he cites the famous passage in John 3:16 that starts off, "for God so loved the world." "Most evangelicals," he said, "hear that word *world* and think it means all the people in the world. But the word is *cosmos*. And it fits with the story of creation in Genesis that God loves his whole creation."

Rusty's emphasis on the relationship with earth is eye-opening. He went on to illuminate a concept I had not known before, that of "general grace." I was aware that most Christians feel a special relationship with God through Jesus, and that this connection is a kind of "special grace" that cannot be earned by deeds but is embodied in the sacrifice of Jesus and can only be experienced by accepting a personal relationship with Christ. But I learned from Rusty about "general grace," which takes in God's love and providence for all of creation. This is the love with which God "so loved the world." It is a general grace that embraces all. So there was room for me in Rusty's universe!

In advance of our conversation, I had decided that I wanted to talk about the hard stuff. I wanted to air the roadblocks each of us encounters as we attempt to bring our own people deeper into partnership in an interfaith project about which both of our communities tend to be notably wary. I decided that it was only fair to be confessional first, and tell him about my problems in the Jewish community with environmentalism, and then ask him about how avid the evangelical community was to hear his message. I essentially told him that the universalism of environmentalism makes some Jews feel that it's not an essentially Jewish issue.

"Even though it's not demographically true," Rusty said, "evangelicals also feel like an embattled minority culture. Our dominant myth is that we're a faithful remnant that acknowledges the truth even though the world has gone in another direction. Until recently, our community viewed environmentalism as a liberal issue, or as a popular fad. But because our theology says that God's character can be seen in the created world, many conservative Christians are beginning to be concerned about creation care. In that view, destroying creation and permitting ecological degradation are like ripping pages out of scripture."

We were really on a roll! I asked him about the pervasive value of consumerism in our culture, our deep hungers of the spirit and flesh. His response was to cite the Jewish practice of Sabbath!

"We have a fundamental addiction to consuming. The Jewish Sabbath is an antidote to that hunger. It helps us test what we can give up from material culture. The Sabbath idea jumps out of every part of scripture; the rhythms of rest and satisfaction and enjoyment of the created order are meant to pervade all of our lives. There are weekly rhythms, and cycles of seven years, and the jubilee cycle of forty-nine years, all celebrating the sufficiency and the providence of God, where we rest and enjoy and encounter with delight the works of God. The Fourth Commandment requires not only *your* rest, but the rest of all of your household, including everyone who works for you and all of your animals—and the land itself. It demands that we not push to the limits our ecological systems or the people who work for us."

Rusty went on to mention that evangelicals generally hold an anti-urban bias that comes from a vision of "our faith as a remnant existing outside of the mainstream of culture. There's an inability to see cities as places that need investment and work, as places to build meaningful community. In a highly urbanized culture we have to rethink our environmental work, conserving not only wilderness or endangered species but also building sustainable communities." He wondered out loud about the value of various Jewish practices, especially Sabbath, which emphasize walkable, vibrant communities, communities that thrive in cities all around the world.

As we tried together to envision a livable urban environment, our minds turned to thoughts of environmental justice. Sources of pollution (diesel fleets, garbage dumps, and waste-transfer stations) are almost always located in nonwhite population centers. Pritchard mused:

"Maybe we need a public policy that puts toxic-waste treatment facilities and landfills only in the zip codes with the highest per-capita income. Systems and institutions can be sinful in ways different than individuals. Environmental issues open a window onto economic and social systems that are unjust and often racist. As an economist, I think our public policies and the ways businesses operate will change once they face the costs of the pollution that they now get to dispose of largely for free. Climate policy may involve getting the right price on carbon dioxide so that it becomes a part of the price of all of the goods that we buy and sell, and therefore implicitly take into account, even if we aren't explicitly looking for the greenest option. It must hit us in our pocketbook. We need to think explicitly about challenging businesses to be not just responsive to price signals and creating value for their shareholders but also to think about ethics in a much broader sense and to allow their business models to be contaminated by their sense of morality and not pretend that there is this huge divide—that businesses are sort of amoral institutions."

I have never felt as safe with an evangelical as I did during this conversation. It was uplifting to find so much common perspective. Yet at the end of the dialogue, I was still a Jew and Rusty was still an evangelical.

I would never have thought it possible for me to forge such a sense of communion with a leader of a faith tradition I feared and sometimes reviled in my youth. But it isn't just me; do a gut-check. Unless you're pretty evolved, there is probably some group out there with a belief that just sticks in your craw. And now imagine finding that members of that group care deeply about something that is very dear to you. Doesn't this prompt a surge of relief, of spiritual joy? I have been saying that religious people can save the environment. But the environmental challenge can save religion right back. If we can find preciousness in our own spiritual tradition and still savor and respect other faith traditions, we will be well on our way to the higher reaches of the mountain of God.

GETTING ABOVE THE TREE LINE

Our democracy separates political power from a specific professed faith. As a member of a religious minority, I appreciate that separation. I follow with interest how faith expressions play out in public policy. Can a crèche be displayed at town hall? Will there be a Hanukkah menorah at the airport? Can the Ten Commandments be posted on the wall of a courtroom? It is an interesting debate, and it reveals witness to an important secular safeguard in a culture where the vast majority of people are self-identified as religious.

I have always been skittish about quoting scripture at public events, and I have been downright fearful when narrow religious agendas are promoted as bases for public policy. But I am all for bringing our passion and numbers and perspective as an interfaith movement to the sphere of public power. This seems safe to me because our passion and perspective are shared across divergent faith landscapes. It is our diversity that makes our message vibrant and strong. The common ground shared by so many is wide enough to bring it safely into the political arena.

Yet leaping into the political arena, no matter how powerful the passion or how important the message, brings it own challenges. If you have ever tried to be a citizen lobbyist, you know it is not a dignified task. Your group basically tries to be numerous and visible by wearing coordinated ribbons and lapel signs. You attempt to grab the elbow and/or the attention of any legislators who are waffling on your issue as they scurry by you in the lobby. You then submit your written testimony—fifty copies, please—and wait in line with the other lobbyists for your two minutes at the microphone or with the senator's aide.

Except when you come with a Baptist choir.

In Connecticut, we were facing an EJ issue—short for *environmental justice*. When an environmental issue makes visible the fact that nonwhite communities suffer effects from environmental degradation more than whites, it becomes a justice issue. Our band of environmental activists had been protesting the so-called "Sooty Six" incinerators that were spewing ash into the six poorest neighborhoods in Connecticut. These plants were fired up on the hottest days of the summer, when demand for electricity was the highest and air quality was the worst. We were against the unmitigated ash dispersal, and for clean energy sources, conservation, and cleaner emissions.

For most of this motley crew of Baptists, Quakers, Jews, and others, it was our first time at the legislative office building in Hartford. Yes, we had our placards and lapel buttons, but we had no patience for the random process of getting the attention of the legislators. Teri took charge. Teri is a Baptist and a gifted musician, among her many other talents. She got out in front of her group and began to sing! Within minutes, an impromptu choir had formed, singing the praises of solar power and God's creation, putting new words to familiar tunes.

This is not a common occurrence at the legislative office building. Not only legislators, but also secretaries, interns, and other lobbyists popped their heads out of their cubicles to see what was going on. The other environmentalists there knew in a flash that our coalition had brought something new to the work.

When people of faith get together to protest something, we come with an infrastructure that is different from most activist groups. We may be *against* something, but we have the capacity to consider what we are *for* as well. We have the stability and perspective to take the long view. We have the vision to see beyond the event at hand. We have a reputation of being perhaps more staid, more mainstream. Perhaps we look more like the people we lobby than some activists do. Perhaps we go to church with them. We as people of faith don't just go to the halls of power, we work there as well. Religious identification is ubiquitous in North America. Most heads of industry and heads of state attend some sort of worship service. More than many activist groups, interfaith groups have multiple points of influence.

As faith-based activists, I believe that we can and should bring not just a position to the policy debate but also a quality. If we have learned well in our churches, synagogues, and mosques, we have learned humility. We have learned to seek collective wisdom. We have learned to ask good questions, to speak our truth, and then to listen. Perhaps we can help foster the conversations between business interests and environmental concerns that will result in workable solutions.

Can I get an *Amen* to that?

3

The New Wealth
Spirit Matters

WHAT IS ENOUGH?

WHAT DOES IT MEAN TO HAVE ENOUGH? What makes us feel comfortable and safe? Is it true or is it a well-worn adage that the best things in life are free? In the Jewish tradition, we say that kindness (social exchange) is greater than charity (financial gifts). Kindness can be exchanged between the rich and the poor; it is class blind. Kindness can be offered to the living and the dead because kindness does not require compensation. We cannot eat kindness, but we can be fed by kind people.

I believe that most people, if they thought about it long and hard, would agree that life can be very rich if we have meaningful work, a worthy purpose, and profound connections. This runs counter to capitalism and our materialistic culture, but I believe that we are suffering as a result of our material wealth. The pollution, the impact on the climate, the waste of precious resources, the isolation, the squelching of sensation and conscience are a heavy price to pay for our version of wealth.

The questions are these: Are we so far from sanity that we cannot get back to it? Is it possible that being better stewards of the earth means having less stuff but more satisfaction? Could we generate an understanding of wealth that includes spiritual abundance and social capital?

OLD MODELS FOR NEW WEALTH

Biblical models for wealth and social wealth—meaningful connections in community—are instructive, even though we are not usually seeking economic theories when we read the Bible. Of course, the economy in biblical times was primarily related to food production, specifically farming and animal husbandry. There was a small "leisure class" of priests in the early years, and they were fed by a tithe of the communal wealth. Later, through taxation, a military draft, and land grabs, a royal class came to be supported, but even then most people tended sheep and grew grain.

Between the various seasonal and annual tithes and gifts, the tax rate for landowners came out to about 20 percent. There were tithes for the poor and the priests, gifts of first fruits, and mandated gleanings (simply leaving the corners of fields and the dropped sheaves for the destitute). No one could really become too rich, and no one could starve under normal conditions.

In the First Testament's Book of Ruth, the story of Ruth and Boaz gives us a glimpse into the economic structure in biblical times. Boaz was a wealthy landowner, respectful to his workers and protective of the gleaners, the beggars who came to his fields to find food. I am reminded of the symbolic stance of the Sufi dancers who whirl in an imitation of the cosmic dance with one hand raised, palm up, to receive divine abundance, and the other hand pointing down to the earth, palm open, to pass that abundance along. That was Boaz's stance: He was overwhelmingly kind to his "beggars"; he seemed to be aware that he and the destitute were both beggars at the table of God.

Ruth was a Moabite princess who was married to an Israelite man and then widowed; her husband had lived with his family for a time in Moab. After his death, Ruth chose the social wealth of family over her upper-class position in Moab, and she returned with her bereft mother-in-law, Naomi, to Bethlehem ("house of bread" in Hebrew). As two unmarried women, they were the poorest of the poor.

Through the institution of gleaning, these two powerless women had what they needed to eat. And through the institution of *yibum* (enforced remarriage of childless widows to single members of the deceased's clan), they were reestablished in the social order as well. Naomi was a kinsman of Boaz, and the *yibum* marriage was arranged between Ruth and the wealthy man. In our era of romantic love (and a 50 percent divorce rate, by the way), this notion is unthinkable and harsh, but in the social realities of old, *yibum* saved countless women from isolation and starvation.

Other terms of Israelite law reveal an unusual view of economics. Lending at interest, for example, was not allowed. Eventually, a system of long-term (fifty-year) loaning evolved, but all remaining debts were released in the fiftieth year. (I know some families who could benefit from this release of debts today!)

In ancient Israelite history, there were also provisions for property. Each family was allotted a parcel of land prior to the conquest of Canaan under Moses and Joshua, and this tribal portion could not be sold. A system of leasing and renting property was eventually devised so people could have some mobility as their means and lifestyle changed, but every fiftieth year the biblically mandated tribal portion returned to the original owner or his or her family. People could not be permanently dislodged from their rightful share. Also, the law was clear that Hebrews could not become slaves permanently. People who had sold themselves into servitude due to dire need were released in the seventh year.

In the current economic downturn, we may well need to turn to such models for a new economy. We may need to choose social wealth over economic wealth. Although it may be a painful process, such choices may bring us some clarity about what we truly need, and we may find that the things that bring us the most enduring pleasure are right at hand.

I think of my daughter's experience. She returned from Thailand with wonderful skirts, colorful scarves, amazing new recipes, valuable memories—and a cracked-open heart. She spent four months with villagers along the Mekong River, which means "Mother of Life" in the local Thai language. All the villagers who hosted her during her stay will be dislocated if a proposed dam project goes in along the Mekong. This is the reason for her cracked-open heart. Most of the places she stayed had squat toilets and bucket showers. There were no garbage cans in the village houses because nothing is wasted. The people she visited live simple lives, gathering their daily bread (or rice) together, plucking chickens, harvesting mangoes, shredding coconuts. Everyone from the *yaiees* (grannies) to the American sisters has a job. They need each other.

It isn't like this in the West because we have the "privilege" of not needing each other! It's funny to think about it this way. All of our specialization means that some people farm, while others fix pipes, and others give sermons, and on it goes. Our interdependence is less obvious to us, and there is a terrible loss in this. It is not hard to "find your place" in a Thai village. Even a tall American girl can find her place in a Thai village. On the other hand, I know plenty of twenty-something college graduates who are still trying to find their place. Sadness, disconnection, and confusion are the downside of our system.

There is an unreachable distance between life in a Thai village and how my daughter lives in the West. Even though she wishes to consume more responsibly, she is sustained by and stuck in many systems that are polluting and wasteful to their very core, all in the name of efficiency. She cannot eat locally because we are not set up to garden and farm in four seasons, or to preserve food from the summer to eat in the winter. She cannot dress locally because no one close by weaves. She cannot eat simply because she's on a college meal plan whose cafeterias are supplied by large-scale corporate farms. The only reason we imagine that our style of food production is efficient is because we do not weigh and measure its many negative impacts: the suffering of the animals; the suffering of the migrant workers; the health costs of the new, deadly bacteria that are endemic to the new means of farming; the carbon emissions; the depletion of fossil fuels used in pesticides, fertilizer, and transport; the cost of farm subsidies that keep certain foods (corn, meat) artificially cheap, to name just a few.

Waste is a sign of wealth. Disconnection from our means of sustenance is only possible in hierarchical and specialized cultures. In a world of subsistence and poverty, waste is inconceivable and social cohesion is life-giving. When people are hungry, they leave no leftovers. Think of our earliest ancestors. They stuck together. They had to, in order to hunt and gather and sow and reap. They needed each other so they had enough. Our material wealth comes at the cost of our social poverty and our environmental precariousness. These consequences are the dark underbelly of what we call wealth.

To engage in an effort of change and repair, we need to imagine something quite unprecedented in history and quite outside of the current way. We need to encourage and empower the spiritual and religious community to show us how to embrace a different kind of wealth.

A LIVING VISION

Ezekiel's vision of the dry bones (Ezekiel 37: 1–27) comes alive for me in this context. His vision of utter devastation and amazing repair is a metaphor for the healing that we need—a divine instruction manual for environmental activists.

This prophet of exquisite imagination envisioned a valley full of dry bones—a difficult image. When I imagine all the ways in which we long for healing, when I imagine all the injustices we yearn to set right—the untimely losses of life, of habitat, of species—I cry, as the prophet did, "Oh, so many. Oh, so dry." (Ezekiel 37:2).

"Son of Man," says the Living One. "Will these bones live?" (Note that the prophet is referred to as "Son of Man," the two Hebrew words that also mean "humanity." In other words, all of us.)

Humbly, and wisely, Ezekiel replies, "You are the one who knows!" (Ezekiel 37:3).

God does not speak to the bones, but commands the prophet to undertake the task. This is our first clue that the divine will requires human intervention to repair these wounds.

As soon as the prophet begins to speak the divine word to the bones, a startling noise erupts, and the bones begin to move toward one another. Here is clue number two for environmental activists: The bones need to be in proper alignment with the other bones. Not everything goes well together. We need to be discerning about which "bone" we are in the body, and who the other bones are that are closest to us in mission and function. It is a very important task to align ourselves properly with our allies.

I used to be pretty unskilled at this. I had some general impression about the need for all of us to work together. All of us *are* needed for the social and environmental repair that is required in our time. But the image of the bones moving into their proper position urges us not to waste precious energy on partnerships that are not well-timed or well-conceived. We all know what that open door feels like when the strong "Yes!" comes through in a conversation. And we all know the disappointment, frustration, and anger that we feel when people whom we want as allies do not yet see the value of partnering with us. Ezekiel is reaching out to us through the ages and urging us to be discerning in this early stage of forming interfaith partnerships.

I think about what it was like as we early faith-based environmentalists sought each other out and began to find language and goals for our shared task. Forming discerning partnerships turned out to be very practical advice. When we listened for the "Yes!" we found a powerful sense of energy—and of relief. Even though we sat in such new and diverse partnerships, there was a sense of coming home, of not going it alone anymore.

The next clue, the next piece of the vision, takes us into the practical details of coordinating and networking. Sinews! Connections! Bones are useless without vital connections. We need to figure out how to operate together. When shall we meet? What tasks shall we take on?

"And flesh rose up upon the bones …" is the next step. How many times have you sat with your allies and said, "Let's flesh this out"? It's funny that this modern idiom for bringing our creativity and good intent and vision to a project—"fleshing out"—is the same image that Ezekiel evokes. Once we're near the right bones and properly connected, we can begin to flesh out our tasks.

"Skin crusted over …" is our next clue. Skin is our outer covering, the face we show the world. Perhaps *skin* is the stage of naming our project or crafting a mission statement. How will we be seen in the world? What will we look like? How will our work be "contained" as it moves forward into the world?

Up until now, the bones in the vision are still lifeless; the action occurred only when the prophet spoke to the bones. At this point, the divine voice intervenes again and gives new instructions. The final step requires us to listen again for divine inspiration.

The Living One tells the prophet to speak to the four winds. In Hebrew, the word for wind, *ruach,* means both "spirit" and "breath." The prophet is to command the living power of the four directions to fill and enliven the dormant forms. And so it is.

There are times when I feel the dry bones of loss and despair about the condition of our environment—and the status of our efforts to change it—in the pit of my stomach. But Ezekiel's vision offers a series of instructions, a repair manual. Shall these bones live? The Living One is the One that knows. But each of us has our part to play.

TOOLS WE BRING TO THE TABLE

Given the consequences at stake, we need to draw on our deepest reserves of energy, imagination, and courage to meet the environmental challenge. There are three tools in particular that people of faith can bring to the table of environmental activism: faith, spirit, and social wealth.

What is faith? Faith is trust. Faith is optimism. Faith is the capacity to work even when we know we will not finish the job. With faith, we can know the worst and work for the best. With faith, we can have pleasure along the journey because we are aligned with a mighty power.

And what do we have faith in? Across the religious landscape, we have faith in a mighty God and an orderly and benevolent universe. The faith traditions of the world can be seen as a sort of owner's manual for the universe. The founders of the world's great traditions taught us, directly, laws for living in alignment with the natural order. And they taught us indirectly by their example. They embodied a simplicity that bears witness to a life rich in spirit. This kind of faith is the daily bread of the spiritual activist.

What is spirit? Spirit is the still small voice. It is the agitation we feel when we are sleepwalking through life, and it is the joyful, wordless satisfaction we feel when we are fully alive. Our sensitivity to our spiritual impulse is the great blessing that we reclaim when we begin to live an environmentally sane life.

It is harmful enough when we are disconnected from where our cans of peas come from, and where the runoff goes from the farms that grow our foods, but it is devastating when we are disconnected from ourselves. There is no way back if we are disconnected from ourselves.

If we cannot feel the urging of spirit, we cannot return from a wrongful course. Remorse and agitation are good for us, if they are the true voice of conscience and the true call to alignment. And the sweet satisfaction of spirit is one of our highest human joys. It is soul food. But we can only have this food when we listen to spirit and let it get all the way from the aura over our heads down to the bottom of our feet, when we act in accordance with the urging of spirit.

What is social wealth? This is community. This is meaningful connection. Social wealth is noncompetitive. The wealthy and the poor can give it to each other. Social wealth is authentic. We can, we must, be our authentic selves in order to benefit from social wealth. We can bring our needs to a conscious community. We can bring our gifts and blessings to a purposeful community. In this kind of environment, we are not judged for having needs. Rather, our needs are the necessary starting point for meaningful contact, for the possibility of giving and receiving.

So much of our day-to-day life is infused with comparison, competition, and the pecking order. We have internalized the hierarchy that pegs us as less valuable if we drive a beat-up car or wear hand-me-downs. Our value, our competence, and our worth are measured by our stuff. Material wealth exists in a zero-sum universe where less is less, more is more, and the laws of physics are very strictly enforced. In the material universe, if I take yours, you have less and I have more. If I have $20 and I give it away, I have less.

But social wealth offers us another view of the human project. If I have love and compassion and give it away, I have much more. Material wealth and social wealth are not governed by the same physics. Rather than viewing ecological efforts as "hard sacrifices," we may find that the very things that bring us the most enduring pleasure are right at hand: a partner, a song, a meditation, a walk in the woods. We may find that it's not so much self-denial to "save the planet" as pleasure: savoring deep, meaningful moments that are more satisfying than consumerism.

We make a huge revaluation of our worth when we move from a framework of material wealth to social wealth, and people don't usually make this transition on purpose. Being laid off might bring a successful businessman to this transition, but it may not be until two years later that he realizes he never wanted to be an investment banker, and he's glad now that he had the opportunity to become a coach or a mentor or an artisan.

Social wealth is not such a blessing when it comes in the form of a pink slip, and I do not mean to be callous about these devastating adjustments that many are forced into in our current economic climate. If we choose voluntary simplicity, we are claiming social wealth. If we are forced into it by joblessness or some other failure of the economy, there is no transformation. There is only loss. But even in the face of loss, we can choose to identify and claim social wealth. If we in religious congregations really value this, we can be a powerful counterbalance to business as usual. A church or a mosque or a synagogue is in the business of building community, and we can initiate, through choice and consciousness, a positive shift in wealth in a time that might otherwise feel only like devastation.

Moving from the material definition of wealth to the spiritual definition of wealth is one of the keys to this environmental action. In combination, faith, spirit, and social wealth can draw us together in appropriate partnerships to be the change agents needed to rebalance our economic structures. We, as the voice of the mainstream, can say to companies, "Do this differently, do this better." We as consumers can choose with our pocketbooks to create a demand for better, cleaner products. We as people of faith have the numbers, the passion, and the credibility to counterbalance rampant materialism. Nothing else is as powerful or as promising as this. Our values implore us to do this. Our numbers make it possible. Our spirit may make it joyous and inviting.

TRANSFORMING BUSINESS AS USUAL

I believe that the transformation of the business world is perhaps the single most powerful effort we can undertake as people of faith to address environmental disrepair.

It seems as if money and materialism have been the enemy of faith for all time, but this dichotomy is not nuanced enough to tell the whole truth. I am hoping that I will not have to live in a cave in order to reach a sustainable level of consumption. I do not think that I need to fast and punish my body to establish a proper relationship between my spiritual and corporal functions. Money is not bad. Commerce is not bad, either. It is, in fact, necessary and delightful to use our gifts and skills to create a product or service of value to exchange with others and to earn our daily bread in this way. Commerce is an essential form of exchange with the material world and with each other.

Yet we need to recognize that the causes of climate change, including damaging forms of pollution, are embedded in the very way we do business. A deep restructuring of our economies is required, and a concerted global effort is needed to make this happen. At the same time, it is not right or responsible for us to point solely to "the corporations" that are despoiling our planet. It should not escape our notice that we ourselves buy their products and hunt for these bargains, even as we are aware that something about our commercial enterprises and our interaction with them is destructive to the environment and not very sensitive or responsive to this environmental impact. Why is this?

We have to start by understanding today's corporate culture. Making the most money possible with the minimum expenditure is the true culture of most corporations. Short-term profit trumps long-term sustainability. It's almost un-American to question this. Corporations generally have an exclusively materialistic mission: They are driven to succeed at making a certain product or selling a certain service, often for the benefit of the upper-level employees and the shareholders. With very few exceptions, large companies foster a competitive culture with little or no reference to larger societal values.

The elements necessary for a corporation to be responsible and responsive to wider concerns are not usually welcome in corporate structure. Within the typical corporation, humility is something people strive to overcome. Not knowing what to do constitutes a sign of weakness, better taken up with a therapist than a boss. An effort at group wisdom is seen as theft of intellectual property. Listening to each other may be kindhearted, but it is often viewed as a waste of time in the corporate world. We only really need to listen to our higher-ups! Listening to ourselves, our peers, and our underlings is fine for the Christmas party, but it is not good for business. Speaking about limits to growth, and the need for sustainability, is just plain blasphemy. Growth is *the* capitalist value. To question the benefit or even the possibility of unending growth is considered unrealistic and soft-minded.

This creates a culture that is rapacious. Mistakes are hidden or denied or blamed on others. Everyone, top to bottom—even the beleaguered customer—is looking out for number one. It reminds me of the first skyscraper, the Tower of Babel, where everyone spoke a different language and crushing destruction ensued.

There are two forces that would compel a corporation without a conscience to become more responsive to environmental concerns, and these tools are in our arsenal. One force is the reality of natural limits to growth. If, for example, a company finds that it is simply using up a fish species faster than the natural rate of replenishment, it *might* adopt a sustainable harvesting policy. Another example is waste reduction. There are a few corporations that are real leaders in this area because they find that using fewer watts keeps their fuel bills down; reusing scrap from the factory floor keeps their production costs down. In other words, a company might choose to adopt a better environmental stance if it helps their bottom line. This is why financial penalties for doing business the *wrong* way are such an important environmental policy tool. Fines for dirty business can level this playing field. We want it to be cheaper for corporations to do business the right way.

The second force that can serve as a corrective for a rapacious business culture is bragging rights. There is a burgeoning demand from consumers (plus legislation) for cleaner, greener products and services. The company that is now reducing its packaging (to save money) or harvesting fish more sustainably (to protect its long-term interests) can brag that it is more environmentally friendly, and that's a good thing. We want to bring together this convergence of market factors and better business practices.

On the other hand, my fellow eco-activists, we need to keep our eyes open for "green washing." *Green washing* means that an organization brags about its environmental track record without actually walking the walk in a meaningful way. I'll tell you my favorite example. I am a breast-cancer survivor, and this disease is an environmental epidemic. Cancer is the biggest medical industry in the world. There are so many financial interests embedded in detecting and treating cancers that many doctoral theses could be written just listing them all. So we now have better ways to scar and mutilate ourselves (our mothers, our daughters), and we now live a few years longer when we get this disease. But few mainstream experiments are under way to study *why* we are seeing so many more cases. Almost no money from any major foundation goes into *preventing* cancer. In the few cases where clear cause and effect have been found (such as yellow dye causing kidney cancer), we see remarkable declines in new cancers when exposure is reduced. And—back to green washing—many of the companies that create products full of known carcinogens are frontline fundraisers for research into cancer treatments! This is green washing: A company that is invested in and profiting from a deadly disease gets bragging rights for helping the poor person who is stricken.

Most big businesses today grow like cancer. They take over new areas and replicate corporate functions without regard to the natural surroundings. They alter the environment to serve their own short-term needs. They ignore the natural limits of the overall system and endanger the long-term survival of us all in their rapaciousness. That is not how things grow in the natural world. In the natural world, plants grow if they are suited to their environment. They grow by reaching maturity and casting off seeds. Their function in the natural order is passed on to the next generation; they do not grow by cannibalizing. The idea of biomimicry— of imitating nature to function well and sustainably—is dismissed by business as usual as "tree hugging." It is not embraced for the sanity and wisdom this approach represents.

Government regulations are not strong enough to pierce this corporate veil. A fundamental redefinition of wealth is in order. The story of the emperor's new clothes, while not a particularly religious fable, comes to mind here. The emperor is naked and only an innocent child has the common sense to say so. The values of our economic culture are naked, and we need to say so.

If all of us at once would shriek from our guts, "This is wrong!" we would have a wonderful start toward letting the old die and allowing the new to emerge. The passion and sheer numbers of people tuned in to their spiritual truth is the only force I can see that is powerful enough for this job. We who claim to be full— from spirit as well as food—can and should name the new wealth, the new health, the new productivity.

IMAGINE THE ALTERNATIVES

We are shareholders and employees and commanders and customers of these corporations, are we not? Imagine the wonderful joy of working together on a goal that is worthy and life-giving. And compare that image to the despair and depression that run like toxins through so many workplaces. *All* of us are suffering from business as usual. It's time to imagine the alternatives.

I don't know what these will look like, but I can begin to venture some guesses. Many of us will be making more of what we need and doing it closer to home. I believe that pockets of relocalization will emerge within this giant global economy. Land use will be more diversified. People will garden on city rooftops and produce energy in their garages. There will be microbusinesses built up to meet local needs, to tap local opportunities and materials. People will barter. Pension plans will be flexible and more reflective of social wealth. Jobs will be shared.

Schools will teach gardening and natural literacy. Recycling, farming, crafting, and energy conservation will be among the big industries. Creativity, communication, honesty, and fairness will be the predominant values in the business world.

My friend Melina has a big backyard with plenty of sunshine. She was motivated last summer to make a community garden of it, and she offered her land for cultivation to various members of her church. The yard now has the gardening plots of six members of her church.

Our congregation has an Internet listserv called FreeBay. People are invited to post on FreeBay if they have something of value that they wish to pass along to someone else. People can also list stuff they need. No money changes hands. When I needed to show my youngest child the "whole world," I received not one, but two globes. I have shared a superfluous TV with a fellow congregant. A guitar changed hands. Houseplants have found new homes. Books have been exchanged. This social network has increased our community cohesion and reduced our clutter and trash.

My friend Vicki has a nice garden, but she travels in the summer. When she is out of town, we are invited to weed and to harvest in her absence.

Another friend, Liz, taught her friend, Janet, how to raise worms. Liz shared a big batch of red worms with Janet, who has turned out to be an excellent worm-tender. Janet has cut her kitchen waste significantly and is the main source of soil-enhancing compost for our extended community.

Churches and mosques and synagogues have figured out ways to build greener buildings and put solar panels on the roof and a composter in the backyard. On and on it goes. Members of congregations give each other rides, which connects the widow with the young family. We feed each other in times of loss or want. We teach each other new skills, which enhances our base of knowledge, saves us money, and nurtures our relationships. Faith communities are in the social wealth business. We can be a powerful voice for reframing the public discourse about what abundance means.

4

Working Beyond Class and Race
Yes, We Do Need to Do This Together

WE NEED TO TALK

IT MAY SEEM OFF TOPIC TO ADDRESS CLASS and racial divisions in a book about faith-based environmental activism. But the truth is, there is very little in the United States that is not deeply affected by class and race issues, and we don't have a history of very useful conversations about this. If we are going to imagine a sustainable environment and economy, we have to answer many practical questions that affect the poor in ways different than the ways they affect the privileged.

Let's start with the obvious: Pollution, toxins, and air quality are worse in poor and nonwhite neighborhoods. Climate change will impact, first and worst, the poor. The problems of drugs, violence, and lack of hope and opportunity are more visible daily quality-of-life issues in poorer communities than the die-off of bee and bat populations. But the intricate web of causes and the impact of environmental degradation is lived there every day.

When we talk about air pollution, we must keep in mind that the poor (both urban and rural) are exposed to more chemical toxins than the middle and upper classes. This problem of exposure is amplified because the urban and rural poor suffer from erratic and inadequate access to health care.

When we talk about sustainable transportation systems that do not pump fossil fuel–based carbons into the environment, we need to think about public transportation. Where are the jobs and how do people get to them if they can't afford a Prius or whatever the next automotive technological breakthrough looks like?

When we think about energy conservation in homes and green building design, we need to work through how tenants of irresponsible landlords will get these services. We need to be aware that housing stock in poor neighborhoods is older, draftier, and leakier.

When we wish to organize as communities to advocate for better environmental policies, we must be aware that African-American communities have suffered through underfunded and short-term programs for decades, and they may be justifiably suspicious of well-meaning white community organizers from out of town.

We need to talk. White and nonwhite activists need to dialogue about shared environmental concerns, and we need to keep these issues out in the open—between us. We need to name them. White people need to name them to show that we are doing our homework, that we are aware of the structural inequalities. And nonwhite or poor or disenfranchised folks need to name them so we can all feel and hear and be aware of the physical and psychological impact of this oppression. Our coalitions must be based on truth and respect. Our shared concerns must be more powerful in our relationships than the obstacles of all these difficult separations. This is not an easy thing to do.

GETTING BEYOND "OVER THERE"

One of the features of racial division, called *structural racism,* occurs specifically within institutions, such as schools and corporations, and results in unequal access to goods, services, and opportunities. But it is not always easily visible to the community that builds the structures. White people with open minds and open hearts may bristle at the thought that they are racist. Personally and psychologically, they may not be. But all middle-class people benefit from structural racism that, by its very nature, is all but invisible. Structural racism lives in many forms, some of them with direct environmental impacts.

Structural racism is alive in the disparity of funding for urban and suburban schools that leaves urban schools resource-poor. This, combined with other factors (distress or chaos in the home, and other impacts of poverty), creates an almost insurmountable barrier to equal education. There is an aspect of the problem that is about personal initiative and there is a structural problem. Some urban schools are unsafe and depressing and seriously under-funded. This is the fingerprint of structural racism. The footprint of structural racism has left an indelible mark on environmental health in nonwhite communities. When we look at environmental impacts and structural racism at the same time, the parcel of concerns that emerges is called *environmental justice.*

Structural racism and environmental impacts are readily observed in the location of polluting industrial facilities. A groundbreaking and eye-opening report from 1987 on environmental racism found that polluting industries, nationwide, are sited with overwhelming frequency in nonwhite neighborhoods, and the trend continues unabated to this day. Polluting industries naturally go to poor and nonwhite neighborhoods to build plants and locate dumps because they can make the jobs argument: "Yes, this facility stinks, but the need for jobs is great here." And these facilities are located in poor and nonwhite neighborhoods because the chaos of poverty already blights the place. As a result, it is highly unlikely that the community can mount and carry out a sustained campaign to resist the industries' infiltration.

On the surface, this disparity may appear to be a good thing for the suburbs. Suburban kids don't have to smell the stink of incinerators and garbage dumps. Suburban kids don't suffer from asthma nearly as much as urban kids do. Suburban property values and quality of life stay pretty high because we don't have all that garbage at our doorstep.

In the long run, however, it is folly to think that pollution is "over there," and, frankly, we don't have that luxury. It is akin to ignoring a cancerous growth because it's on a toe that we don't use too much. Toxic pollution affects those closest to it first and worst, yes. But soil, water, and air are all global phenomena. The air in the first-ring suburb is just a little better than the air downtown. And in some heavy commuter towns, such as those around New York, where moms and dads whiz off to big jobs in the city, asthma rates are just as high as asthma rates in the South Bronx.

I do not say this to minimize the plight of the poor. I say this because our work as environmental advocates is not a charity. Let's be realistic: We are in this for self-interest. If I am engaged in this battle to help someone else, there is a real possibility that I will go home if the battle gets too protracted. If I am in it to help myself, I'm in it for the long run.

The truth is that if garbage-transfer stations were located in the lush suburbs, we'd have a lot more powerful voices speaking to their legislators about precycling, recycling, and better methods of waste management. If we had vinyl and pesticide production going on in the suburbs, we'd have many more people advocating for new, less toxic chemicals and greener building materials.

The practice of shunting deleterious environmental impacts onto poor communities is dampening the coalition building necessary to effect change. If suburban whites see it as "not my problem," and suburban blacks see it as "one of my many problems—but not the most pressing one," there is no logical constituency for change. Add to this dismal state of affairs the fact that there are very few coalitions for meaningful, mutual exchanges between classes and races in America. The philanthropic model of "us" helping "them" creates distance and defensiveness on both sides. We need to stamp out this paternalism. As long as we think the problem is "over there," we're not ready for partnership.

FINDING COMMON CAUSE

Every denomination, class, and race has environmentalists in their midst. I have observed, however, that there are faith communities that have an additional layer of identity wrapped around their religious affiliation, be it race, or immigration status, or some other minority group marker. I call these groups "ethnic churches," although many of them are neither ethnic nor churches at all. These congregations may be places of cultural refuge or community organizing in addition to serving as places of worship. I am thinking of urban churches that are dealing with gun violence, or mosques where many members are relative newcomers to the United States, or Polish Catholic parishes that are serving a dwindling cadre of elderly immigrants, or Jewish communities that serve their congregants educationally and culturally, as well as in a strictly religious idiom, and so on. These types of communities have particular needs, and it is likely that global climate change is low on their list of concerns.

I believe it is our responsibility, as faith-based environmental organizers, to find common cause with these less-well-represented communities, if we can. To do so, we must ask ourselves: Why is our environmental work relevant to this congregation? With the many concerns of this congregation, why is our environmental ministry of interest to them? This community may profess the same love of God the Creator as our other allies, but the environmental questions are an exercise in finding common interests. The search leads us not across theological divisions but rather to the divisions among class, culture, and ethnic groups. This line of questioning is very valuable because it draws our attention to the connections between creation care and love of neighbor.

What *are* the connections between environmental degradation and human misery, unemployment, violence, health, migration, and isolation? How *does* the work of our environmental associations support human dignity and safer communities?

If we cannot see the answers to these questions, our environmental work will remain largely a white Protestant phenomenon. Our issue—environmental stewardship—will compete with other important charities and causes for time, energy, and resources. We need to recognize that our social and our environmental problems are interwoven. A mentality of disposability and disconnection undergirds them both. And the strategies necessary for healing our social and environmental problems are the same: inclusiveness, treasuring diversity, and human dignity. We do not have enough time, resources, or energy to address these issues separately. We need to get to the roots of these concerns in order to effect transformative healing.

When black community activists think about safe neighborhoods, we need to share their concern. We need to think about lead in the paint of crumbling buildings and sickening air pollution—as well as getting guns off the street. When black community organizers talk about safe, affordable housing, we need to include in our equation energy-efficient dwellings that are more affordable to heat and illuminate year after year. When nonwhite activists speak about the need for good jobs, we need to think about sustainable, dignified jobs that pay a living wage *and* green-collar jobs that contribute to the abundance and security of our ecosystem. How can children grow up with a sense of awe and wonder about themselves and this precious earth when their physical environment is a crumbling mess?

Education, hope, and dignified jobs must be part of our concern as faith-based environmentalists. The preciousness of each human

life—not just the preciousness of habitat or endangered species—
must motivate our work. We need to rethink what ensuring food
security means. It's not just a matter of sending trucks of food daily
into poor neighborhoods; real food security requires an infrastructure that supports locally grown food to meet regional needs. This
solution also results in a reinvigorated industry, community development, and cultural cohesion.

Local assessments of real needs and real solutions will be a
powerful tool in creating more vibrant and more sustainable communities. We need more diverse land-use patterns, and we need
infrastructure development and a diversity of housing stock. We
need more energy auditors and solar-panel installers. We need
more insulation and window installers. We need more centers for
recycling and reuse of goods. All of these needs are opportunities—
for new jobs, more connection, and less waste.

We must look deeply into the roots of and solutions to our
environmental challenges in order to forge real common cause
with people across class, cultural, and ethnic lines. And the only
way to get it together is *together*.

WORKING TOGETHER

When I set out to write this book, I wanted to tell you about the
many nonwhite and interracial faith-based groups that are working hard together on environmental issues. I wanted to tell you
that we in the interfaith movement have overcome the social separations, but, instead, I need to tell the cautionary story. I need to
share why it is so important for us to work beyond class and race
and what some of the pitfalls are that we'll have to face.

In my experience there are a limited number of interfaith environmental groups that function well between race lines. There are
many individual Hispanic, nonwhite Muslim, and African-American
environmental activists, but there are only a few congregations

within these communities that are organized and active on environmental issues. The environmental coalitions that are truly diverse center on environmental health; this is becoming a pressing issue in urban faith communities.

But there are individuals and local groups who are succeeding in working beyond these class and race boundaries. Many of them have environmental justice, health issues, and affordable housing as their points of shared concern. I have asked a treasured colleague to tell his story of working together across race and class lines. Rev. Woody Bartlett, who hails from Georgia, was an early member of the Interfaith Power and Light movement. He was on the fund-raising committee, not because he ever did fund-raising but because he "prayed on it," and a few of those grants he prayed for came through. I asked Woody to share his story because he is from the South, a place of historically proud and empowered black church leadership. His story focuses on the challenges and the requirements, as well as the rewards, of cross-community organizing.

The Great Light Bulb Swap of '06
BY REV. WOODY BARTLETT
Founder, Georgia Interfaith Power and Light

There I was on a Saturday morning in November, precariously balanced on a small ladder, burning my fingers on hot, 75-watt incandescent light bulbs, trying to get them out of rusty old sockets in the hallways of poor people's apartments in a public housing project in Atlanta, Georgia, and the thought went through my head, "How in the world did I get into this?"

The story goes back years, and it involves grace and commitment and a deep desire to help poor people. Mix into that a determination to bridge the deep gaps in the racial divide in the South, as well as preserve the earth from the folly of humans that is leading us toward catastrophic climate change, and you find me on that ladder.

Three organizations collaborated on the effort: Georgia Interfaith Power and Light, an organization that my wife, Carol, and I had founded several years earlier; Antioch Baptist Church North, an African-American church of considerable size and clout in Atlanta; and the Georgia Power Company, the main public utility in Georgia. The connection with Antioch was key. The man at the center of that connection was Deacon Joe Beasley, head of Antioch Urban Ministries, Inc., Antioch's outreach arm to the poor and the homeless.

I had heard of Joe during the 1970s, well before I met him. He was often in the news, protesting some injustice or another. You could always count on him to take the side of the poor and marginalized. And they were often positions that I, nor hardly any other white person in Atlanta, could join in on. We might sympathize with Joe's position, but the politics of the time meant we would be too far outside our base of support to comfortably be part of it. We could easily become marginalized ourselves and lose whatever power and influence we might have. It was an all-too-familiar dilemma.

The South, like many other parts of the country in those days, was deeply divided along race and class lines. Slavery and segregation had left a heavy toll. The races never got together in any meaningful way. People of different races did often work together at their jobs, but the end of the workday meant the end of contact. That was true particularly of Sunday mornings, when a large majority went to church but on a strictly segregated basis. It was often said that Sunday at 11:00 a.m. was the most segregated hour of the week.

But the divisions weren't just racial. There were deep class and economic divisions also. Economics often did bring the rich and poor together, but only as poor people did the unskilled labor for rich people. That, obviously, did little to break down the class divide. It was ironic that, at the same time, there was a thriving black community in Atlanta, studded with a large professional class and populated with a surprising number of black millionaires. But there were very few easy ways for black and white professionals and people with money to connect.

It was a situation that fostered suspicion, ill will, and no small amount of anger. And the standoff prevented many important things from getting done—improvements in education, health care, the introduction of business and industry, and, last but surely not least, improvements in the environment.

In the early eighties, I took the position as the canon for community ministries of the Episcopal Diocese of Atlanta. I was the church's agent out into the community, particularly concerned about poverty. And the concern for poverty translated into much more connection with African-Americans because they made up the bulk of people in poverty, as well as a significant number of those who cared for the poor. In this new position I could much more easily publicly stand for justice, and did so from time to time. I was also the director of the Episcopal Charities Foundation, a small grant-making arm of my office. We gave money to some pretty interesting poverty ministries, not all of which were related to the Episcopal Church.

Then I met Joe. That year he was the president of the Christian Council of Metropolitan Atlanta. I was working on a ministry that was sponsored by the Council, so we would end up in meetings together and got to know each other. He was a quiet, soft-spoken man, but with a deep, festering anger when it came to society's treatment of the poor. There he gave no quarter.

Sometimes I could join him in a position that he was pushing. Sometimes I held back. But we did develop a trust, and he did come to know me as someone who cared for the plight of the poor, representing a church that cared as well.

I learned that he had retired as a sergeant from the U.S. Air Force. I also learned that he held an affinity with the prophets of old, for he would often deliver a scathing rebuke to some group in authority for their negligence of the poor. Occasionally, I found myself in the target group. It was not always very comfortable.

Still, Joe and I retained a working, if not affectionate, relationship. Then in the nineties I took a job with a nonprofit organization that was making a serious effort to get the most chronically homeless people off the street and into housing with support services. Joe's group, Antioch Urban Ministries, came to the table, and we worked together on a project. Unfortunately, the project never came to fruition, but we did give it a solid push, and through that, Joe and I grew closer.

After retiring, I continued to do some work on poverty and homelessness but turned my attention increasingly toward my deepest love and deepest concern—the way we humans were despoiling the creation. It threatened my children and my grandchildren. And it threatened the poor most immediately.

In 2003, Carol and I founded Georgia Interfaith Power and Light. We did it because the organization promised to directly address global warming, arguably the greatest immediate threat to humans. We did it because we were deeply connected to the faith community; it was our natural alliance. And we did it because, as Carol said, "I just love the name!"

We recruited an energetic Steering Committee, which started quickly. We got a small gift to buy some compact fluorescent light bulbs (CFLs) at wholesale prices. We borrowed a nifty display gadget from one of our church members. It had been created to demonstrate to officials at the Coca-Cola Company the benefits of CFLs in energy savings. It had a standard electric meter and two sockets. We put a regular incandescent bulb in one socket and a CFL in the other. People could see that the two bulbs gave off the same light, but the meter ran so much slower for the CFL. The demonstration turned into money in the viewer's head. Our garage became a warehouse. Huge eighteen-wheeler trucks pulled up in front of our house and delivered bulbs. Sales soared. We were off and running.

In our deliberations, the Steering Committee pondered from time to time the impact of energy on the lives of the poor. But we knew of no way to address our concern. There were still deep divisions between the races. For instance, there were no black people at our table, nor at any other table that we knew of.

Then the Georgia Power Company forged an agreement with the federal Environmental Protection Agency to distribute free CFLs to individual customers across the state. We happened to be talking with some officials from Georgia Power when we asked the question, "Would it be possible to focus some of these giveaways on the poor?" They said that they would be glad to do that if we could come up with a workable system. We agreed to try.

I talked to the head of the Atlanta Community Food Bank, Bill Bolling, and he said that since all their distributions were to agencies dealing directly with the poor, they would canvass a dozen of those agencies for ideas. They sent out a letter. And who should reply but Joe Beasley, my friend at Antioch Baptist Church North.

I called Joe and went over to his office to discuss the idea. He said that he had already installed CFLs in his home. He was a believer and eager to do what he could to help. He gave me a tour of their operations. Emergency assistance food distribution was under way. There were lines of people, dozens of volunteers, stacks of food all over the place. It was pretty impressive. We also walked down the street to the church's community housing corporation, which was redeveloping some of the blighted properties in the immediate neighborhood. They had come a long way since Joe and I had first tried to do that project for the homeless. I was impressed again.

Then we sat down in his office to talk about possibilities. We could distribute light bulbs through Antioch Baptist Church's emergency assistance program. But Joe had a better idea. Right across the street from the church was a large public-housing project. He called the president of the tenants' association, and she said that they would love to have some more energy-efficient bulbs in their complex. We went across the street and talked to the property manager. He thought it might be a good thing, too. And he was especially taken by the notion that the complex could save up to 75 percent on lighting costs by installing those particular light bulbs.

Several days later we went down to the headquarters of the Atlanta Housing Authority and discussed the idea with the people in charge. They, too, liked the idea. Meanwhile, the property manager at the housing complex was counting lightbulbs. It turned out that we could use 3,500 of them. I called Georgia Power with that number; they gulped, did a quick count of inventory, and agreed to supply them.

When Joe and I first talked about this idea, he had said that a great prospect for doing the actual installation was the Saturday morning men's prayer breakfast. Could I visit and explain what we were proposing? So one Saturday morning I did. There were some fifty or sixty men there for breakfast, prayer, and moral support. Rev. Dr. Cameron Alexander, pastor of the church, was there. I knew Cameron from my days when Joe and I had tried to do the housing deal.

Laypeople led the gathering. There was prayer, Bible reading, some testimonies—and the one white guy with his meter, explaining what we would be doing during the great bulb swap. Their hospitality was warm, particularly as Dr. Alexander ribbed me about not understanding all of their ways because white folk usually just didn't get it. Cameron's talk to the men was pointed, quite earthy, and very inspirational. His remarks and some later comments by some participants confirmed what I had heard, namely, that Antioch was perhaps one of the prime churches in the community in pulling young black men back into responsible membership in the community. It was all quite moving. We ended up picking a Saturday several weeks away for the bulb swap.

The Saturday arrived, clear and crisp. The light bulbs had been delivered the day before by Georgia Power. We started at Antioch with more prayer and a hearty breakfast. And then, at about ten o'clock, we went across the street. The property management company had called for volunteers of maintenance workers from their other properties so there were about a dozen of them. And the tenants' association had publicized the event so there would be few surprises as we went to the various apartments. We divided up into small teams and set out for various sectors of the complex. There were three of us in my team. The maintenance worker would approach the door, knock, and holler, "Maintenance." If someone came to the door, we would go in. If not, the worker would open the door with his passkey. If the family was at home, we would have a brief discussion with them about what we were doing, how it would help them financially, and how it would help the atmosphere. We together hoped God would be pleased with what we were all doing. Every encounter I had was pleasant and respectful. It was a joy.

Except, we had not thought about bringing gloves or a rag for hot bulbs. And few of the volunteers had brought a stepladder. So there was often a tedious balancing on rickety chairs, and there were burned fingers. Still, we pressed on. Meanwhile, as the teams were inside, the property manager of the complex was constantly going around outside in his little golf cart, bringing new supplies of CFLs where needed and taking away bags of old incandescents. It was quite an operation.

About one o'clock we were finished. We went back over to Antioch for a lunch of fried chicken and cole slaw. It was delicious, particularly after 3,500 light bulb swaps.

As we counted up what we had accomplished, we figured that, over the life of those new bulbs, we had saved more than $130,000 in the cost of utilities and replacement bulbs (CFLs last about seven times longer than incandescents). And, at the same time, we had saved more than 2½ million pounds (1,250 tons) of carbon dioxide from the atmosphere, again over the life of those new bulbs.

Perhaps most important, we had demonstrated that the poor and those who care for them really do care about the creation. We found out once again that workable alliances between those who have the light bulbs and those who have contact with the poor can get a great deal done. Divisions in class and race can kill those efforts, of course. Still, those divisions can be overcome through long-term, individual relationships built on mutual respect and trust.

To heal the planet, we must build those relationships.

GETTING TO THE TABLE

Woody's story exemplifies some of the experiences that I have had in cross-race community organizing. We often do not sit at the same tables. Suspicions and stereotypes abound on both sides. People just think that "*They* don't get it."

This is all very frustrating and discouraging to me because I approach interracial community organizing with every good intention and a drive to be inclusive. But my authentic, friendly, mutual relationships with a few nonwhite colleagues are new and fragile.

Relationships are based on working together, not just on church or family or neighborhood. Woody's relationship with Pastor Joe was tested in the fire of failures and successes. It developed over years. The light bulb project required the full, empowered partnership of several all-black institutions. Each had to go to the "table" of the other. They had to be good guests in each other's worlds. They had to trust each other enough to tease each other; that is, to get past the awkward stage of politeness. The project would not have succeeded without wide partnership and mutual trust and respect.

To develop new environmental allies and work together effectively, white and nonwhite activists need to unlearn so many prejudices. We need to exercise new social skills in addition to our skills in environmental activism. There is an opportunity in this to heal social and economic wounds along with environmental injustices, and it can begin with a few core steps:

Go to the Table Together

Show up. Visit. Meet each other in places of shared concern. I met one of my treasured environmental allies at a meeting about public safety. This young man's life had been affected by gun violence, and our shared interest in safety became the touchstone for our relationship.

Listen

One of the unexamined attitudes of white privilege is the subtle sense that whites know the questions and the answers, that we are here to "help" others "get it." This is not the attitude of mutual partnership. To develop new partners, we need to be humble and authentic.

Share your concerns and listen. This goes both ways, for white and nonwhite potential allies. If you hear concerns at a gathering that seem naïve or far from your truth, say so. Invite an open-ended inquiry to what shared interests there are, if any. Be truthful about how high a priority this is for you; don't create false expectations and then simply fail to follow through.

Because we know that we are making a conscious effort to overcome natural social separations (different neighborhoods, races, or cultures), our environmental activism is a perfect opportunity to learn more about the reality of environmental degradation. Inform each other. Listen to what is unique and pressing in the other's understanding of the issues.

Work Together on a Manageable Task

Lasting relationships are based on many points of contact. Having a job-based friendship or liking the same recording artist is a weak basis for a working partnership. It is an opening, at best. Be aware that when you share a common mission to bolster the environment for the good, you are building a partnership. Each meeting or event is another link. One of the most effective ways to build a partnership is to work together on a doable project of mutual interest and benefit, one that can generate tangible results, such as Woody's light bulb project. Build time into those opportunities for the relationships to grow. Eat together, worship together, and take breaks together. Shmooze. Take delight in each other's company.

Imagine the children of Israel at the foot of Mount Sinai, reaching to hear the divine word from Moses when he came down from the mountain. As they stood in a circle, each and every one of them had a slightly different perspective. Yet, they stood together, tolerating that tension, because they were all reaching for the same goal.

None of them could have the comfort of "knowing what to do." And how our minds seek that sense that we're in control, that we're sure of ourselves. In order to create a transformation of our environment, we will need to tolerate a great deal of "not knowing what it looks like." Humanity has never been in this position before and none of us, alone, knows what can be done and what should be done. We need to learn how to cultivate collective wisdom.

I believe that religious environmentalists can help create the conditions, the petri dish, where these kinds of dialogues between diverse interests will emerge. It is a delicate thing to create this kind of dialogue, but it is also simple, if not easy. People with divergent positions need to feel safe to speak truthfully about their legitimate self-interest. Any groups meeting to talk must be reminded of the value of listening, and it must be clearly stated when listening has become difficult or blocked. In this situation, the common good and the shared interests must be restated so the discourse can get back on track. Patience is required until the group wisdom and consensus begin to emerge.

It is disarming—and powerful—to speak from this position of humility. Not only are the right words required, but the right attitude as well. An attitude that invites disparate views and allows us to say, "I don't know exactly what should be done, but I care deeply about our children's future. How can we move forward together to balance these interests?"

We have an extraordinary opportunity to honor God each time we meet at the table across class and racial divisions. We bring our minds, our hearts, and our hands together to repair our own broken society and the earth we share. When a Jewish scholar, Dr. Abraham Joshua Heschel, marched with Dr. Martin Luther King, he said his "feet were praying." Those of us who feel called to care for creation understand that the only way to do this is in ever wider coalitions. The richness of our new partnerships is a reward unto itself.

5

How Big Is Your God?
Theology Meets Earth-Care Activism

DIGGING DEEPER

THE ENVIRONMENTAL CHALLENGE IS UNIFYING; that is to say, we will sink or swim together. But it's not enough to examine how our actions can save the planet; we need to examine our way of thinking and our beliefs, because these motivate our actions. We need to examine what we've been taught about God in light of today's environmental crisis. And we need to dig deeper into the roots of our faith to see whether it has more to teach us about earth care than we previously might have thought. As people of faith, we need to begin asking these faithful questions:

- What do I believe about the relationship between God and creation?

- How do I see my relationship with the rest of creation, my life as part of creation?

- What does my faith have to do with the environment?

- How can my faith guide me in my environmental actions?

At this current juncture of self-inflicted calamity, we need to ask ourselves these fundamental questions once again. Questioning and examining ourselves and our faith in relation to the environment are crucial new tasks for individuals and religions of the world to undertake. It's time for Bible study groups and Torah classes and Qur'an discussions to become environmental classes as well. Responding to the earth crisis may be just as important as—or, better yet, part and parcel of—responding to the Commandments or the Gospel or the Law or Dharma.

I asked my friend and colleague, Rev. Tom Carr, to share with me his theological reflections and questions that confront him as an earth-care activist. Tom is an American Baptist pastor and has been a part of the National Council of Churches Eco-Justice Working Group. He has studied concepts of the new cosmology with Sister Miriam MacGillis of Genesis Farm in New Jersey, and he is on the board of SmartPower, a national clean energy advocacy group. Tom is also a founding member of Connecticut's Interfaith Power and Light affiliate, the Interreligious Eco-Justice Network.

Tom was an early, vocal, and passionate leader in the efforts to clean up power plant emissions in Connecticut, and environmental justice has been a central part of his ministry for many years, even as he serves a thriving congregation in West Hartford. One of Tom's congregants once said, "You *always* talk about the environment," which he insists isn't true, but he always speaks from the new cosmological understanding of the human place and purpose in the universe that he has grown to embrace. I value his way of opening our eyes to a new understanding of personal faith in the larger context of the cosmos.

❧ The Big Context
BY REV. TOM CARR
Cofounder, Interreligious Eco-Justice Network of Connecticut

During the first couple of decades of my life, no connection was ever made, in church or at home, between my Christian faith and the earth and ecological responsibility. That all changed for me in 1987 when a barge of garbage became famous. The Mobro 4000 floated up and down the East Coast, and then down to Belize and back, looking for a place to dump nine tons of human waste. At the time, I was a pastor in Ohio, and I first learned of the barge story on the evening news. The first night, the broadcaster was chuckling about it, but I found it shocking. The second night the story ran, it was treated with more seriousness, and I found myself asking, "What does my faith have to say about this?" That question started this whole journey for me.

There were no immediate answers. I was not aware of the many articles and books being published, or lectures being offered, concerning religious faith and ecology. Scant attention was paid to the Assisi conference—an interfaith gathering that was one of the first to present care of creation as a shared religious value—hosted by Pope John Paul II in 1986. My personal exploration led me to the Psalms and Genesis and hymns to find the imagery of God in "nature," and to hearing all of them anew, but none of my colleagues were thinking about these things. I did remember that a seminary professor of mine had done some thinking and writing about ecology in the sixties but had since moved on to other theological issues.

I felt alone; I was doing my research alone. But I soon discovered several of the mystics, from my own Christian tradition and others, along with many insights of aboriginal peoples, and I began to reread what the early church fathers wrote about nature and the cosmos, along with some of the Jewish thinkers of that time. They all had profound insights into nature and human nature and the interconnectedness of life.

I realized that I, too, had always had a sense of wonder, an innate sense of the grandness and collectivity of us all. My parents and grandparents, particularly my dad, had a practice of seeking out what was the essence of a person or situation. Whenever my dad would engage in conversation, he would try to discover what it was that really mattered to the one with whom he spoke. When it came to the essential human values, he always got to the heart of it.

For instance, growing up outside Detroit in the 1960s, I experienced firsthand the racial tensions that dominated those times when everything was seen, literally, in black and white. Our church was quite involved in the dialogue between black and white congregations that was alive during those times, and my dad ran an interracial youth basketball league. I remember the things he would say and do when it came to how we were to act and interact with those who seemed so "different" from us. His way was to cut right to our commonality, to what was shared by us all, in effect forcing us to see what it was that united us. My mother, then a teacher, volunteered as a tutor in the inner city and would go into kids' homes, even during highly charged moments of racial tension, because she believed that education was the great leveler and unifier of people. My family attempted to live the connections and relationships as part of our faith tradition. We were not overly concerned with anything related to the environment in any way, but our faith and practice went well beyond prescribed theological doctrine, Baptist though we were.

In my late teens and early twenties, I went through a period of spiritual exploration that led me into connections with a very conservative, exclusive group of Christians during my college years. They believed Christianity was the only way, that all other faith traditions were wrong, misguided, and missed the mark when it came to knowing God. But I had a wise pastor at that time, and when I was home from college, I would talk with him about all of this. At the time, I was considering which seminary to attend, and some of my conservative friends were trying to make sure I "had it right." My pastor would listen to all my reasoning and tell me, "Tom, those are fine seminaries, but consider how you were raised, the values instilled in you from your family and your church." He urged me to remember the broader and more inclusive ideas that had always nourished my soul.

He was right, and I enrolled at Colgate Rochester Divinity School, an open-minded, progressive seminary that showed me the call to justice and taught me how to think broadly, understanding the big-picture universe of God. My theological education gave me the intellectual and spiritual tools to treasure my tradition and to continue the process of seeking commonness among us all.

Expanding Universe, Expanding Theology

Moving from an exclusive mind-set to a more inclusive theology is a process. As I was clarifying my thoughts for this essay, I remembered reading the book *Ishmael* by Daniel Quinn, a novel where a gorilla becomes a tutor for a young man trying to expand his way of looking at life. Though I've come to put aside much of Quinn's thought, the book did help broaden my worldview at an important time in the evolution of my intellectual and theological reflections. Shortly after that, I came across *The Hidden Heart of the Cosmos* by Brian Swimme, and Thomas Berry's *The Dream of the Earth* and their cooperative effort, *The Universe Story,* all giving me the beginning of a language for making sense of an expanding universe and the human place and purpose in it.

As part of a sabbatical reflecting on the new cosmology and Christianity, I spent a week at Genesis Farm in New Jersey, where Miriam MacGillis led a group called "Exploring the New Cosmology." There, I went beyond what I had read in books and began to know, spiritually, at the level of the heart, how connected everything is and how I am part of everything. As poet Joyce Rupp says in her book *The Cosmic Dance: An Invitation to Experience Our Oneness,* "The soul of the world and our own souls intertwine and influence one another."

During my time at Genesis Farm, I was sitting with Miriam and some others when one person wondered, "How am I ever going to remember all of this?"

Miriam replied, "You know this. You are the story. You won't remember every detail, but you know it because you are it."

This personal and theological journey has led me to the expanded worldview and the means of activism that are central to my life right now. I consider the earth as the context in which all other issues play out: racial and economic justice, gender, poverty, war and peace, to name a few. I am beginning to grasp that these are the subsets of the larger earth context, and that the major reason the planet's life systems are collapsing is because our contexts are too small.

Our conscious identity may be as humans or as Christians or as Americans, but what we are first and wholly are living forms arisen on planet Earth. Because all life is one, injustice against humans is injustice against the planet, and to harm the planet is to harm all beings that are alive here.

Yet, because we are part of a culture that believes in radical individualism and separateness, this interconnection between all living beings often slips out of our consciousness. We fail to see things as they truly are, in their proper relationships. This failure happens, I am convinced, because we continue to look at life through our old lenses, a worldview that I pray will be transformed quickly for the sake of earth's life systems.

Currently, we have what has been called a "use mentality," where all life is for human use and consumption. Think of some of the language we use: *natural resources, human resources.* Resources are things to be used by humans while all else is "other"—stuff for our consumption and economic benefit.

When the first President Bush was campaigning for reelection in 1992, he made a stop in the Pacific Northwest amid the strong lumber interests where environmentalists had been raising concerns about destroying old-growth forests. Rather than acknowledging the connectedness of life, the president framed the issue as an "either/or" choice: people or the spotted owl; jobs or the environment. That's a false choice. Everything is connected: no environment, no jobs; no earth, no people.

Part of the reason Western civilization embraces the idea of separateness is science. The modern scientific method grew out of the belief that the observer could step away from the observed and measure it in an objective way. In this way, the observer is understood to be totally separate from whatever is being measured. Our legal system is designed with this in mind as well. We say we want "just the facts," as if any observer of an event were totally objective. But we cannot do that in any definitive way. We now know that we affect everything we observe; absolute objectivity is impossible. Our observing demands our participation, and that affects every situation. In fact, Einstein called the idea of separateness "an optical delusion." There is no such thing as separateness; all is one.

That brings us directly to the amazing discoveries of today's cosmologists and quantum physicists, which, at first glance, may seem a long way from our questions of faith and the issues of environment but, in fact, offer us a radical new way to see how they are intricately connected.

The New Cosmology

Every person, culture, and religion has a cosmology; it is a way of seeing that orients us to life as we find our place and purpose in the universe. A cosmology is the sum total of all that we give meaning and value to, as well as how members of a culture view the origin and nature of life. It is the foundation for exploring and seeking answers to questions fundamental to life: Why is there something rather than nothing? Where is God in this vast universe, and how do we relate in a consciously self-aware way to the Sacred? Where do we "fit" as a species in this vast cosmos, and where do I fit? What makes life meaningful? How are we to relate to other humans and all the other living beings who share this planet with us? What happens when we die?

One of the "cosmological powers of the universe," to borrow a phrase from mathematical cosmologist Brian Swimme, is cataclysm. By *cataclysm,* I mean that as much as the universe is constantly bringing forth new life, growing, changing, and always moving toward greater and greater complexity and fecundity, it also constantly destroys parts of itself, usually in violent ways. The largest cataclysms on earth are, of course, mass extinctions. We now know that, in earth history, there have been five major extinction spasms. The greatest of these occurred 250 million years ago at the close of the Permian age when 70 percent of all land species and 95 percent of all marine life were wiped out. Gone went most of life on earth in the blink of a geological eye. The most violent of all cataclysmic events in the universe are the supernovas, when gigantic stars explode, obliterating everything within millions of miles around them—stars, solar systems, small galaxies. But out of those cataclysms come life. Our own solar system is the result of a supernova. Out of the violence was born the only solar system to have given birth to life, as far as we know. In fact, we are literally stardust.

Cataclysm is both destructive and generative. Consider the story of Noah's ark and the great destruction of the flood. Everything was decimated but a small remnant of life. The world was radically changed through this massive destructive event. Yet, the divine impulse moved forward through the covenants with Noah, his descendants and all the creatures who came out of the ark, as well as the covenant with Abraham. Later, during the Babylonian exile, the Judean kingdom was totally destroyed. And yet, two generations later, something brand new emerged, the seed of rabbinic Judaism. A small remnant of Jews returned from exile, and the next stage of the culture of Judaism was born.

We see this over and over again as each new stage is connected to the past, contains elements of the past, and is thrust forward through the cycles of destruction and new life. Like the supernova parent of our solar system, which brought forth primary elements necessary for life, earth, all her creatures, and we humans continue to rework and reshape those elements as part of the cosmological powers of the universe.

Cataclysm contains within itself both death and resurrection, and it is both part of the story of the universe and part of my faith. As such, this part of the story of the universe is wide enough to hold my Christian story and the cosmic God. What if we understood the crucifixion in light of cataclysm? Here was Jesus—rabbi, healer, spirit-person (to use a term I first heard from Marcus Borg in his book *Meeting Jesus Again for the First Time*)—who had begun a new movement within Judaism with a small but growing number of followers who caught his spirit of a way of God and a way of living that were life-giving and brought hope. His central teaching involved the kingdom of God that had been inaugurated in his coming—which was a dangerous teaching because there was only one kingdom at the time, Rome. But his teaching was what his listeners knew in their souls to be true, that God's ways were not Rome's ways and that to live in the kingdom of God was to reject the claims of Caesar. This had to be liberating, exciting, and frightening to anyone who heard his words and saw what he did. And Jesus certainly knew that his way would sooner or later conflict with the "powers that be," both Roman and Jewish. And they did, culminating during the Passover season in Jerusalem when he was beaten, humiliated, and killed on a cross, the instrument of

Roman power and death and a deterrent to anyone who would dare attempt anything of the like.

Cataclysm. The whole world of those first followers was shattered, wiped out. All hopes and dreams for reform and renewal were gone. But three days later, his followers experienced his presence with them once again; they knew that he had risen and was living with them in a different way. And his presence carried within it the spirit of the past and moved them into a brand-new future.

Death and resurrection. Destruction and new life. At the very heart of Christianity is one of the cosmological powers of the universe. In a single human being, an expression of life as it is in its fullness is revealed. For me, this interpretation of the meaning of the cross is so much more powerful than a set of doctrines to believe to make me right with God.

In a worldview of radical individualism and separateness, perhaps sin is imagining ourselves to be separate from God and/or anyone and anything else, and then attempting to live out of that separateness. But how in this one living universe can we be separated from anything and anyone at all, let alone our Creator? We can imagine ourselves separate. We can try to disconnect. But we can never cut ourselves off from the web of relationship that is the universe.

The Web of Relationship

In previous eras of human history, we understood humans to be radically separate from all other living beings and "above" earth and her life-giving processes. And the majority of Western industrial societies still see the universe this way. But we now know that we are part of a great unity, a physical, psychic, spiritual existence in which everything is connected to everything else. The new cosmology allows us to see our human place in the universe, based on the discoveries of scientific cosmologists and quantum physicist of the twentieth century and the wisdom of many cultures and religious traditions. Some 13.7 billion years ago, everything was bound together in a compact ball of energy, but with the cosmic flaring forth at the beginning of things (the Big Bang), there came the differentiation we experience today. But we remain expressions of this essential oneness; we are part of a web of relationship. There are no separate parts—if by *separate* we mean unconnected objects or a collection of objects that, when linked together, comprise the greater whole. All is one.

In light of this, cultural historian and Roman Catholic priest Thomas Berry has said that we are at a moment when we need to "reinvent the human, at the species level" as we seek to discover what our place and purpose is in life. What has become evident to me over the years is that to think clearly about these primary issues underlying our theological reflections, we need to be intentionally situated at the intersection of science and theology. How we live the answers to these questions now that we know this earth, who is herself an expression of the universe, will make all the difference in the world for the planet, for our species, and for us as people of faith.

It is crucial for us to remember that earth (the universe, in fact) is the primary and largest context. All other situations, social and cultural organizations, and issues are subsets of the larger context. This is a much broader way of looking at things than we usually imagine, and it directly confronts the problem: our contexts are too small because they don't take into account *all* of life of which we are a part, which makes for a theology that is too limited.

Today, science is showing us what people of religious faith have long confessed but usually forgotten: that human beings are primarily planetary creatures and only secondarily part of particular cultural, religious, or national groups. In classical civilizations, people defined themselves by their tribe or religion or culture. And these definitions remain valid today. Yes, we are Americans, engineers, Republicans,

Christians, Jews. But all of these are secondary to our larger, primary identities as planetary creatures, intertwined with and alongside all other living beings.

I can only speak for my own faith tradition when I say that, for many Christians, the identity of being Christian takes precedence over everything else: They see themselves as Christians first and only secondarily as human beings who are creatures of planet Earth. But our identity as Christian, as essential as that is, emerges from our identity as human beings, a much larger enterprise. And being human is derivative of yet the even larger context of being part of life.

This moves us, I believe, to the question of where is God in this vast physical, psychic, spiritual universe. In short, I believe that God is everywhere, the One who may be approached in all things and through all things but who will always be, should the universe expand forever or end in a big "crunch."

> Where can I go from your spirit?
> Or where can I flee from your presence?
> If I ascend to heaven, you are there;
> if I make my bed in Sheol, you are there.
> If I take the wings of the morning
> and settle at the farthest limits
> of the sea, even there your hand shall lead me,
> and your right hand shall hold me fast.
> —Psalm 139:7–10 (NRSV)

Other psalms proclaim that God is the God of the hills and stars, the void, the light and the darkness. When we consider a plant or a blade of grass or the wind, we are experiencing something of God. Each living being is a mode of divine revelation, an expression of the Sacred in life. And so, we should be very clear about what we are doing when we mindlessly or intentionally destroy species of life: We are eliminating vessels through which God is made known. Surely a person and a plant are not the same as God or the other. Differentiation is as much of this universe as is unity (or "oneness," as I like to think of it). There is amazing diversity in life, vast differentiation. However, in the end, all is one. It's this sameness—this being with and being of all that is—that is so inviting to me because it is so true of the God in whom I "live and move and have my being" (Acts 17:28, NRSV).

Jesus offers a prayer in John's Gospel where he asks that we may all be one, as God and he are one (John 17:20–23). The church has always understood those words to mean that God and Jesus are one and that the church should be unified, without internal discord and division, in order to do the work of God in the world. And that's very good. But I hear this prayer today in an expanded way, for not only is the church called to live out its essential unity, but all people are called to be consciously aware that all life is one. It is the unified whole from which each individual differentiated whole emerges.

Consider a Russian nesting doll. Each complete doll exists within the others and all of them make up the whole. They all "fit" within the others. They *are* the whole. But if you remove one of the individual dolls, it just doesn't quite fit together; the whole is incomplete. Distinctly unique and yet one. So, too, are we unique creations and yet embedded within everything else. The universe is a vast unity of an amazing diversity.

A New Way of Understanding

Like the quantum physicists who recognize that all life is interconnected, or better yet, that all life is a web of relationship, oneness is the primary truth of all existence. Each religious story is a reflection of the larger cosmic story, and all faiths are part of and emerge from the universal oneness. This truth is something I believe the mystics of all faith traditions understand and know so well. When I read a Sufi mystic or a Jewish mystic, I hear the deepest truths of my Christian story in their words. I sense that what I know about God is shining through them, reflecting the great singularity of life.

Of course, the particularities of our specific traditions matter; they matter a lot. But the problem today is that we focus so much on the particularities and uniqueness of our own faith that we lose sight of what we have in common—which is almost everything. In fact, we can't survive without each other and all the rest of life. We are part of life, reflections of reality, and the truth of the matter is that though we are unique, distinct beings, we are one—part of the "implicate order," in the words of physicist David Bohm.

So, if we return to Jesus's words in John's Gospel that "I and the Father are one," I understand him to be saying, "not the same but one." Even today, despite the choices and the amazing discoveries of scientific cosmology, quantum physics and the beginnings of a new cosmology, how could Jesus have described the great unity and great connection that he knew any other way? Words fail us here because we are speaking of a connection beyond the intellect, one that can only be known through the contemplative heart and the eye of wisdom.

If, as the Christian faith believes and is stated in John 3:16, "God so loved the world" (*world* = *cosmos*), then those created in the "image of God" (Genesis 1:27) should love the cosmos, too. And that involves both "how" the world works and "what for." Religion and science go hand in hand. Faithfulness is not about blind belief; quite the opposite is true. Wisdom does not require parking your brain in the vestibule of the church when contemplating God and nature, and shelving science when its findings conflict with specific doctrine. Faith is the ability to be in awe of the wonder of life and the sacredness pouring through it all. Faith is sight, a "seeing" of the sacred nature and reality of life in which God's presence flares forth everywhere, in every living being.

My real concern is that we will continue in our blindness and not see the universe the way it really is, that, out of some misguided form of piety, we will not listen to what the earth and scientists and environmentalists are teaching us. If we refuse to bring our religious reflections forward in light of a new cosmological understanding of life, then our notions of the God who calls us, the creation, and our relation to it will become outmoded antiques, museum pieces, gathering dust on a shelf.

There is so much hunger for truth and spirit and life on our planet! People are starving for deeper connections. Yet many people these days—and I can only speak about Christianity—are separating what they know scientifically, mathematically, and philosophically from what they believe about Jesus, God, and the church. They create a dualism, setting aside the deepest truths of their souls when they put on their "religious hats," seeking to escape to another world, the afterlife. What a loss! What a misunderstanding of religion's message, crying out for integration.

When we do this, we get into an unimaginable bind, where faith and piety become a denial of science and reality and, ultimately, we lose our place on earth. And when we "lose" earth, the deep neurosis begins that so infects our culture today. We need to be reading and reflecting on this, to start talking about a new worldview—clergy with their congregations, religious education teachers with their classes, individuals with their peers. None of this is too "heavy," too overly scientific to understand. In fact, this is something we are yearning for! None of this replaces what we've always known and cherished, but it means we can bring those insights forward into a new era as we continue seeking the truth of life.

I am convinced that religion, rightly rooted in its context and reflecting truth, can be a powerful force for corrective environmental action. Religious communities can play a central role in the ending of the old and the birth of what is yet to be. We have long recognized what even some scientists are now saying: that we live in a physical, psychic, spiritual universe, and that everyone, and everything, is holy, a mode of divine presence. In every area of life—how we structure our societies; build our cities; grow and harvest food; develop our economies, and our educational and legal systems; arrange our forms of government; what we do with toxic wastes; how we organize our health care systems—the way we understand our connection to all of life is of fundamental importance to devising a way of life that is mutually enhancing for all.

Environment Magazine ran a cover story in 2004, asking whether religion can save the environment. I think we have to understand that ecology—this study of wholeness—can save religion, too. The diversity and complexity of the cosmos is the context and the model we can emulate in this important time for the reformation of religions all over the world. If we can nestle our truth in the natural order, like the Russian nesting dolls, we will have a vibrant faith, a relevant faith with an important message for our time. This encompassing theology is the filter that will allow us to see what we are doing to this planet and what it really means for our future, our *near* future. With our hearts and our minds in the right place, we will act differently on behalf of earth's integrity.

The past can guide us, the foundational stories of our faiths can guide us, if we recognize that our understanding is always evolving. It is that evolutionary view to which science and all the rest of life calls us. That is my prayer and my hope: to have the courage enough to let the old way of understanding die and allow the new to be born in us.

6

The New Eden
Reclaiming the Garden

SEEDS OF POSSIBILITY

TWO REMARKABLE WOMEN—one Jewish and one Catholic—are reclaiming our original occupation as gardeners. They continue the work of Noah, who saved the beasts and the seeds in a time of destruction. They are pioneers who see their activities as a form of sacred and restorative justice. They are giving us, literally, the seeds of a new possibility. It is really an old/new way because it builds on the collective intelligence of millennia of humans and even more millennia of natural evolution of seeds.

Modern agriculture has concentrated and altered the gene pool of the most important products to such an extent that indigenous and diverse species of wheat, corn, and other life-sustaining crops are on the brink of extinction. This is more important than it sounds. As many as 15 percent of adults have an allergy or a sensitivity to modern wheat, according to Foodintol, a website that tracks food intolerance. This means that they are sickened by and cannot eat the food that has sustained our ancestors for millennia. This also means that the vast majority of our wheat crop is genetically the same and would be vulnerable to the same pests and climate conditions.

Diversity offers resilience, and there is very little diversity in today's agriculture. Yet today, agricultural practices prize uniformity and efficiency above all else. There are pluses in this system—the center of this country, the breadbasket, can feed the world—but there are costs and losses, as well. Our current system entails a spiritual loss, a loss of wealth of human heritage, as well as a deep desensitization to the seasons and cycles that sustain us.

We also become desensitized to where our food comes from. Our mechanized production results in cheap and efficient grain that is often "dumped" into the market by selling it for a price that is below market value. This practice makes local foods more expensive in comparison. It squelches indigenous farming even more, and puts more and more people, especially in developing countries, into dire dependency and poverty.

This efficient and uniform way of gaining our daily bread is also heavily dependent on fossil fuel. The nutrients needed to replenish the soil are derived from petroleum products. Enormous expenditures of diesel fuel are used to farm with heavy machinery, to process and package food, and to transport it many thousands of miles to the grocery shelves.

Efficient large-scale farming is desensitizing in another way. We have all heard of "factory farming," which we imagine to be, maybe, crowded conditions for animals. But the truth is much darker, much worse for the animals and for the vitality of the food system. Animals are altered, bred, and fed in a way that makes them gain weight quickly. (Perhaps we ourselves are reaping the consequences of that in our burgeoning obesity.) Cattle are fed corn, which is plentiful due to federal subsidies and a network of rails, but corn is not their natural diet. The conditions of an altered diet and extreme crowding, resulting in constant exposure to feces, has contributed to new and alarmingly resilient germs that are appearing regularly in the human population. For this reason, animals are fed a constant stream of antibiotics, and meats are processed with decontaminants that are themselves toxic. All this takes place not on the family farm, but on a new place called, ominously, the CAFO, an acronym for Concentrated Animal Feeding Operation. This is not a place to go on a class trip. It is marked by terrible conditions suffered by animals and workers (many of the desperate undocumented folks) alike.

The critical environmental questions we face are these: Can we reclaim food production for the life-giving, local, community activity it once was? Will churches and synagogues start orchards and four-season gardens on their lots? Will we feed each other fresh, seasonal food, as humans have for centuries? Or will we over-tax the breadbasket and create a gigantic, fragile food system that could be destroyed by a single organism or a sudden shift in temperature or rainfall, as predicted by climate change models? When will the diversity, the vitality, and the compassion come again into the food system?

I want to introduce you to two women who are showing us that there is a way not only to bring sustainable agriculture back to our communities, but also to put poverty prevention in our hands by considering the bigger implications of our food systems.

First, meet Elisheva Rogosa. I met Eli at a conference in rural Vermont, and I loved her so much that I started to bring groups of teens from Hartford to rural Vermont to expose them to the simpler ways of farming she espoused and practiced. At that time, Eli was writing a curriculum with an outfit called FoodWorks, which was crafting a gardening-based elementary school program. Everything from math and science to literature and history was built around gardening and what they called "foodways" to capture the sense of community, place, and history that is part of the culture of food. This curriculum was crafted into culturally nuanced versions, and a Hispanic, a Jewish, and an Arabic curriculum were eventually added to the original New England curriculum.

Eli later relocated to Israel and helped establish the use of the gardening curriculum both in the West Bank and in Jewish Jerusalem.

She once said to me about the Israel/Palestine conflict, "Everyone wants this land, but not everyone seems to want it under their fingernails." Her idea was that if we love the land, we should work it. If we feel rooted here—Jews or Arabs—we should sustain ourselves from the soil. She eventually became an advisor to what she described as the "largest Palestinian civic association," an association of gardeners and growers. She advised them on organic techniques and alerted people that many of the agricultural chemicals were being misused by Palestinians in dangerous ways because the warning labels were written in Hebrew. I always thought it was astonishing that this observant Jewish woman could establish such meaningful relationships and gain such trust from her Palestinian colleagues. Obviously, her humility and sense of service were palpable. Her utter kindness trumped all political identity and cross-group suspicion that marks so many of the relationships in that tense part of the world.

I visited another of Eli's projects once in Bethlehem. She had developed a relationship with a Bedouin farmer, Daoud (Arabic for *David*), and helped him go organic and better conserve his water resources. Daoud had reworked the piping in his simple home so that water first hit the food preparation area and then headed to the bathroom to be used as "gray water," that is, for flushing. From there, the water was piped into a series of settling tanks (just what they sound like) where the solids floated to the bottom and the water, a little cleaner, seeped into the next holding area. These tanks needed to be emptied from time to time. Next, the water went through simple plastic tubes into a kiddie pool set into the bone-dry foothills of Bethlehem in Daoud's backyard. They had decided on a bunch of water plants to cast into the pool and, according to Eli, "Hyacinth won." That is, the hyacinths liked the climate and the nutrients, and they flourished in the little artificial wetlands in Daoud's backyard. The hyacinth leaves were fed to the goats, who shared a large open pen with free-ranging chickens. When the water left the kiddie pool, the bacterial content was so low that the water was well within the range allowed for agricultural water. It was used, via drip irrigation, to water Daoud's vegetable crops. Every drop of water in that desert was used four times in a system that would cost a few hundred dollars to replicate. Daoud was even thinking of trying to run the water through another tank to grow tilapia on his farm, but the political realities overtook him, and he has not been able to do that yet.

Over time, Eli became aware of the depletion of seed diversity that affects farmers all over the world, and she went on a mission to reclaim these seeds.

℘ Wheat Sheaves and Matza Tales
BY ELISHEVA ROGOSA
Founding Coordinator, Heritage Wheat Conservancy,
Waterville, Maine

A few years ago I baked matza for the first time in my traditional clay oven-*taboun,* carefully following the *halachot* (laws), mixing deep and quick, rolling it out thin, then baking it in the scorching hot oven, all in under eighteen minutes.

I expected to make a crunchy, hard matza, like the ones shipped out from the Brooklyn matza factories. To my surprise, my matza was soft, like a thin pita. Although it was kosher for Passover, I wondered why this was not like the "real thing." What had gone wrong?

I have since learned that soft matza *is* the "real thing," the traditional matza baked from generation to generation until 1888 when Dov Behr Manishevitz, from Cincinnati, perfected a mechanized press to crank out industrialized matzas. Today, soft matza is known as Sephardic matza, after the Eastern Jewish communities who were not modernized by Dov Behr's invention.

I tried to find native Israeli wheat to bake with. After all, at the dawn of agriculture, the first wheats evolved in the land of ancient Israel. Every Israeli schoolchild knows that wild wheat—called *Em Ha Hitah* (Mother Wheat)—was rediscovered by Aaron Aaronson in 1906 growing on the windswept hills of the Galilee. Search as I did, I was not able to find Mother Wheat anywhere; nor the *emmer* grain (sometimes mistranslated as spelt) that was used in the original matza in ancient Egypt. I could not even find native Israeli wheat for sale in Israel. Nothing. Bakers and suppliers nationwide explained that our wheat in Israel is imported from Midwest megafarms, with not more than 15 percent of locally grown wheat mixed in. Even that 15 percent is a transplanted modern variety, bred for high yield and uniformity for the global food industry.

Alarmed, I met with the director of the Israeli gene bank, our national repository of southern Fertile Crescent indigenous seeds, to discuss the situation. Are there any native Israeli wheats available today? Her response was troubling. Israel's native wheats are on the verge of extinction. Although the gene bank does store a small collection, these ancient varieties were collected decades ago, many have lost vitality, and vast populations of indigenous ancient wheats have never been collected.

I remembered a wonderful wheat researcher I had met at the Iowa Seeds and Breeds conference for conserving heritage seeds, Abdulah Jaradat, a Jordanian, now a senior researcher with the USDA. His countenance had lit up when we discussed ancient wheats. I contacted Abdulah, who in turn contacted colleagues in the Middle East. Apparently, Jordan and Palestine buy 90 percent of their wheat from Kansas, too! With trepidation, I e-mailed, then called my unknown neighbors. Their response was so warm that, without thinking it through, I invited them to meet at the Israel gene bank to discuss our shared problem. Incredulous as it sounds, *they accepted.* The Israel gene bank was thrilled and helped raise the funds. Palestinian researchers agreed to join us as well. Bravely, I covered the hotel and travel expenses for our honored guests from my modest farmer's pocket, asking for contributions for an organic banquet at the Adam and Eve Permaculture Farm in Modiin. We were on! I announced the meeting to wheat colleagues from Europe. France asked if they could join us.

November 29, 2007, Jordanian, Palestinian, Israeli, and French wheat researchers, coordinators of gene banks, traditional farmers, and rabbis met together to discuss our shared loss of biodiversity. Indigenous seeds know no boundaries. We established a regional project, Restoring Ancient Wheat, to collect and exchange our remaining ancient wheats before they are lost to the world. We are rushing. Time is short. The few ancient wheats left are grown in remote villages. Families save a few dinars by buying the cheaper U.S. wheat at their local markets, while the farmer who grew up farming with his parents now looks to the city for work. The community heritage of rural farming is as threatened as the ancient wheats.

Loss of heritage wheats is a worldwide, silent crisis. Just as the monocrop of genetically uniform potatoes in Ireland was wiped out by a strain of blight in 1845, modern wheat, the most widely grown crop on earth, is a teetering monocrop, bred through a genetic bottleneck like a pedigreed inbred racehorse: high-performance but unstable, a disaster waiting to happen. Unprecedented global warming looms menacingly over modern wheats, fine-tuned for predictable weather patterns, for push-button, computer-controlled harvesting spanning thousands of acres.

I submitted a paper to the European organic breeding conference on the "State of Seed in Israel and Palestine." In it, I surveyed our critical loss of biodiversity and outlined strategic steps to build cooperation. Not only was I invited to present the paper in France, but I also became the Israeli representative to the EU organic cereals project and cofounded the Landrace Wheat Working Group.

Luckily for us all, I found the ancient *emmer* that nourished biblical Israel right in front of my nose, in the *Machanhe Yehuda* open-air market in Jerusalem!

"Do you know what this is?" I asked Abraham the shopkeeper, incredulously.

"Of course, it is *aja*," (Amharic for *emmer*) replied Abraham with a gleeful smile.

"Abraham, this was the wheat used for our first matzas in Egypt!"

"Yes, it has been kept by our people in Ethiopia."

"Why don't you grow it here to bake matza?"

"Ah," he explained sadly, "who of our people have farms here in the Holy Land? And who would buy our simple foods?"

Delicious *emmer* wheat nourished ancient civilizations, but today it is almost extinct. It has survived as an important food in the remote Ethiopian highlands, tended and preserved by the very peoples who themselves were almost lost. Most Ethiopian Jews were farmers until they immigrated to modern Israel, but today they cannot compete with high-tech Israeli farming.

From generation to generation, for thousands of years, Jews have been baking bread and matza. Every Jewish home was once redolent with the fragrance of fresh-baked bread. Baking matza was a family experience. With the burgeoning interest in artisan breads baked in wood-burning ovens, and the awareness of the value of biodiversity and organic farming, let us restore our heritage of ancient wheat and artisan breads and once again taste the delicious flavor of the real thing.

Now meet Andrea Ferich. This woman has a fully realized view of environmental justice and social justice in a deeply Catholic idiom. The Catholic Church is such an august and majestic body of the faithful; it is the oldest and the largest church. The church has a distinguished commitment to human dignity, diversity, and quality of life; it is an important voice on environmental justice. And this one sweet woman in Camden, New Jersey, is bringing it all together in her bicycle-powered community garden in the poorest part of town. Listen to how she reclaims her sacred calendar and her mandate for justice in her groundbreaking (literally!) development of Eve's Garden in one of the most blighted spots of Camden.

❧ Communion Agriculture
BY ANDREA FERICH
Founder, Eve's Garden, Camden, New Jersey

In one of America's most dangerous and polluted cities, I have found myself in a new Eden, growing a community and an economy supported by sustainable agriculture. Being a farmer in Camden, New Jersey, has opened my eyes to the interconnectivity of the rituals of the Catholic Church and the acts of growing food, following the same yearly rhythms, the same seamless liturgy, as acts of eco-justice. The rhythms of the earth and the calendar of the church form our traditions in this new Eden. We come together around the calendar, attuned to both agriculture and justice, to break bread and harvest potatoes as the Beloved Community of God with all of creation. These are acts of peacemaking and earth communion.

Our bread can be peacemaking or it can be warmaking. Our bread can be communion with the land or it can fuel the empire. When industrial agriculture converts fossil fuels into food, using an entire gallon of gasoline to grow a single bushel of corn, there is war on the land. The current politics of food are not acts of eco-justice. The average American dinner plate of food travels 1,600 miles, and two-thirds of our domestic waste is food packaging. In the global context, farmers in "less developed countries" are required to follow policies that violently suppress the organizing of the people, policies that don't allow seed saving, and policies that require the growing of cash crops.

The earth speaks in a still, small voice when we draw near as garden keepers. My journey as a farmer began beside my mother in the garden. I have learned from my mother what she learned from her mother, tracing a matriarchal lineage of herb and vegetable knowledge to my Native American grandmother. I visit the woods of my childhood and ancestors along the Susquehanna River. It is the land of my mothers beside the streams where they lived and the land that they planted. I walk these woods with my brothers, and I am soothed back into the forest with the songs of the sparrows. It is the forest of my vision quests and walkabouts, preserved as an heirloom that is saved. I remember the stories of my mother and her mother's mother. This forest grounds me to work for eco-justice. Here in these woods I lament that everyone does not grow up in the forest. The lament of the city is in a sacred balance with the whispering of the forest. The light and the darkness are the parts of the sacred rotation, our seasons, our seed, and our harvest.

I understand my place in the Beloved Community as a farmer not only through being in the forest but also through my intellectual pursuits. I received a degree in ecological economics from Eastern University to understand the true cost of the American dream, the effects of overconsumption on the ecosystems of the world. In the rain forests of Belize, I studied tropical ornithology, agriculture, streams, and forests, fully immersed in a wild and beautiful life of creation brought to life vividly in those rain forests. It nurtured my seamless love for the earth and my Creator. As we studied biblical scripture, I came to read the holy text in light of my ethical understanding of sustainable agriculture as an act of eco-justice, and as a prayer that draws me close to the good news that Jesus spoke.

Reclaiming the Land

After my semester in Belize, I returned to my college campus eager to make a difference for eco-justice. There I heard Father Michael

Doyle from the Sacred Heart Parish in Camden. He spoke as a farmer-priest from Ireland who loves the land, who knows that it is inherently good, and who finds inspiration in puddles and children's eyes. He spoke as a poet who points to peacemaking from the pulpit and the pasture. In particular, he spoke about the poor and the land of Camden that are dumped on decade after decade. He spoke of how unemployment, abandoned houses, and prostituted land and air are overtaxing the poorest of the poor.

Camden is similar to Nazareth, the birthplace of Jesus: They are both dumped on by the empire. People say that nothing good ever comes from Camden; the same was said of Nazareth. In Camden, the earth is very broken, and so are the bodies of many of the people. The idling diesel trucks stop at every corner, raping people's lungs while picking up prostitutes in a land that itself has been prostituted.

Camden cannot take any more polluting industry. The Waterfront South area is home to the county sewage treatment plant, the county trash-to-steam incinerator, the world's largest licorice-root processing facility, a cement factory, numerous scrap-metal facilities, hundreds of thousands of rumbling diesel trucks, two state Department of Environmental Protection Superfund sites, twenty-eight U.S. Environmental Protection Agency contaminated sites—and my farm. Neighborhoods like Waterfront South are where all the unwanted waste goes, where the social landscape is often one of prostitution and desperation. Yet Waterfront South is home to so many amazing minds and loving families, home to farmers from other lands, and generations of people who come together in the kitchen. It is a place where we can create home, break bread as a community, and practice resurrection with fierce imagination. Certainly, the economy must be rebuilt here, and sustainable agriculture is an avenue for ecological, economic, and social health. We need to reclaim the land here in the belly of the beast.

When I first moved into a community house (similar to a Catholic worker house) in Waterfront South, my community partners and I reached out to many of the surrounding industries to begin brainstorming ways to reclaim industrial waste as a resource. When we approached the trash-to-steam incinerator operator, we asked the managers if we could take the excess steam that they were releasing into the air and use it in a closed-loop system to heat a greenhouse. We were all very excited about this idea. The company even committed $10,000 toward purchasing a greenhouse, a place where the children and adults from Waterfront South could grow their own vegetables and flowers.

I then approached the Heart of Camden, a local housing organization started by Sacred Heart in the 1980s (when more than 50 percent of the houses in the neighborhood were abandoned), with a proposal to be under their nonprofit auspices. They graciously offered me a job as the greenhouse manager under the Family Services Division. But then we encountered our first roadblock. We received word from the trash-to-steam incinerator that the company's lawyers would not allow the children to come to the greenhouse if it were on their property, but they would still give us $10,000 for the greenhouse.

I spent a lot of time in prayer, walking around during the next few weeks, talking with residents, and exploring alleyways and abandoned spaces. I stumbled on a corridor of alleyways at the heart of a residential block, across the street from Sacred Heart Church and School, which connected the school, three different neighborhood streets, and a preexisting neighborhood garden. One afternoon I walked to this garden to borrow a hose and, while wrestling with the tangled hose, the padlock for the garden gate slipped from my belt loop. I looked all around and just couldn't find it, so I sat down and prayed for a moment. In the silence I noticed a large, vacant, trash-strewn lot directly adjacent to the current garden. I knew at that moment that I was looking at the future site of the greenhouse.

The next miracle in making the greenhouse a reality came in the form of a visitor one rainy night. At the community house we often open our doors to feed and listen to the needs of the people who live on the streets, often prostitutes in this prostituted land. When we first met Eve, she was soaked and looked sickly. As we were sitting in the kitchen watching her eat a large, warm plate of food, she told us that she was greatly relieved to be off the street. At our table she opened up and, when we asked, shared some of her favorite pastimes. To my excitement, she said that she liked to garden. A few days later I found Eve again, and we walked around the corner to a patch of grass along the street and pulled out weeds and spread our wildflower seeds. In the few months that followed, I gardened with other children and adults in the neighborhood and returned to see the germinated flowers. Eve shaped my imagination. The greenhouse and gardens, dedicated as "Eve's Garden," evoked our new Eden of eco-justice in Waterfront South.

Each act in our garden subverts the economy of the empire. We started seedlings in the backyard in cold frames made from found trash, planting in the compost that we made in an old trashed refrigerator. We sprayed wildflower seeds out of Supersoaker water guns. I walked with one of my community members to the contaminated Superfund sites near our house and threw handmade compost balls filled with white clover seed (a legume known for bioremediation) over the fence to reclaim the land that had once been a tannery.

Our neighbor, Miss Flossie, lived in the only other occupied house on the block. She was being fined for the unkempt "weeds" in her side yard—which I identified as lambs quarters, an edible green three times higher in iron than spinach. We harvested the weeds and shared in the reclaimed feast.

We now grow more than twelve thousand heirloom seedlings a year—and grow imaginations that take over the neighborhood with beauty and a deep connection with the earth that is inherently good and wise. At Eve's Garden, nobody plants alone. Planting is our communion with the earth. Bread is our communion with each other. We built a bread oven made of a material called cobb, a mixture of clay, loam, straw, and sand—all locally collected materials. The children helped a wonderful natural builder named John Fox construct the bread oven without any power tools. We mixed up the cobb ingredients with our feet to make our own bricks and passed the bricks down in assembly-line fashion.

When the fire is burning inside the oven, it appears as though the flames are coming out of a mouth. The bread oven itself is a sculpture of a forest creature's face beside a tree. The sculpted tree acts like an armature that holds up the timber frame roof of the bread oven. The roof is a "living roof" of growing sedum, lavender, sage, and winter rye. We fire our bread oven once a week beside the greenhouse and cook "seed to table" meals for the community.

The children still buy junk food from the corner stores, but we find ways to intercept their decisions. I am so grateful when I see a child carrying a bag of sunflower seeds. Many of the children like to eat them, and their imaginations are engaged when we go to the garden and stand beneath the towering sunflowers that we planted and harvest the seeds from gigantic heads. We harvest the sunflower seeds the ways the native people did, a process that often leads children into the transformative "ah-ha moment." They are captured by the transformation of the sunflower, from seed to flower to seed, "Oh! Sunflower *seeds*!" We cut the sunflowers from our garden to be placed in the sanctuary for the Feast of the Transfiguration (August 6) in commemoration of the time when Christ was transfigured on the mountain with Elijah and Moses. We also cut the sunflowers to lament the bombing of Hiroshima on the same day. We have carried the cut sunflowers to Camden City Hall and placed them at the door of our city's chief operating officer, laid as prayers to end the annihilation of Waterfront South. Our ecological liturgical year re-creates a culture around healthy celebration and food.

Ecological and Liturgical Seasons

Just as the earth rotates around the sun, creating the ecological seasons from seed to harvest to table to seed, so too does the Catholic Church year cycle around saints' days and feast days, creating the liturgical seasons of Advent, Epiphany, Lent, Easter, Pentecost, the Transfiguration, the Assumption, the Feast of the Holy Cross, and the Immaculate Conception, and return to Advent. The feast days celebrate a certain grounded timelessness, connecting us back to traditions that are based around the seasonal rhythms of agrarian culture and folklore. The feast days become our sabbaths, a period outside of work, time, and the global economy.

Seamless intimacy with the ecological seasons and the liturgical seasons unites the practices of the church and the earth into the seasons of the eco-liturgy as one rotation of seasons. It is within this economy of love that we save and grow seeds at Eve's Garden throughout the liturgical seasons, following the sun in the sky. Many of these traditions are like umbilical cords that nurture us with the wisdom of our ancestors deeply connected to the earth.

Certainly, the spring is one of the most exciting times for us in the garden. We plant our potatoes in the garden on St. Patrick's Day. We fire the bread oven that we made from natural materials and cook these potatoes when they are harvested on June 16 for Blooms Day. We create our own folklore with characters such as the Mulberry Princess as we follow her clues to the ripened mulberry trees in the beginning of June. We follow pirate maps found in fishermen's bottles that lead to the buried treasures in our garden. It is a miracle in "America's Most Dangerous City" to find ourselves surrounded by great wisdom and the creativity of the margins. We are filled with the energy of the children in a world of uninterrupted play. In our gardens we commune with the goodness of the earth, the saints and traditions that have gone before us, and the rituals that allow us to intercede for the world.

On March 25, nine months before Christmas, on the Feast of the Annunciation of the Virgin Mary, the day of Angel Gabriel's visitation announcing her pregnancy, we plant the marigolds for our garden, waiting in expectation for the glory they will bring for the Feast of the Assumption of Mary in August. To the Mayans and other indigenous peoples, the marigold is full of various medicinal uses and meanings as a holy flower. The marigold serves a variety of purposes in our garden. As the plants of red, yellow, and orange swirls begin to grow in the greenhouse, they are transplanted out into the garden where they will each grow for a member of our congregation. In addition to their beauty, the marigolds also serve as companion plants for pest control with the tomatoes. We grow hundreds and hundreds of marigolds for the Feast of the Assumption of Mary. The crop of marigold heads, worn as Mary's golden crown, is brought to Sacred Heart Church in the middle of August for the feast day, and they adorn our statues, our parishioners, and our altars in a feast of gold on August 15.

Mary, who became the vessel for the birth of Jesus, was herself conceived in purity—the process we call the immaculate conception. The Feast of the Immaculate Conception of Mary, the day of celebrating the purity of Jesus's grandmother, comes right as we have finished harvesting our seeds for the year. As I understand this feast day, it is a celebration of the abundant life within Mary's womb as she conceived, the miracle of her reproduction, and the life of Jesus within her. During the last couple of weeks before the Feast of the Immaculate Conception, we save the heirloom seeds from plants that we have grown and bless them on this feast day in December.

Seed Saving as a Model for Eco-Justice

A certain paradigm shifted for me while saving seeds within the paradox of Camden. It is upside down, like the ways of the mustard seed in the global economy. Like the parable of the mustard seed from the teachings of Jesus, which tells of the smallest of seeds blooming into a large, beautiful, and potent plant, we were seeing the tiniest of seeds in our garden bring life-changing results to individual lives, to the way we ate, to our community, and to our faith. The process of seed saving was becoming our communion with the ground. When we planted seeds in the "Promised Land," when the soil got under our nails, we loved the soil; we loved the life it brought. We were becoming humans of the humus, like Adam of *adamah,* the Hebrew word for "earth."

The process of growing, watering, and gathering the seed every year also helps me understand the mysterious transformation of the body of the seed as a parallel to the mysterious transformations of the body of Jesus. The seed-to-wheat transformation is just as miraculous as the Holy Eucharist, during which we receive the bread and the wine that are transformed into the body and blood of Jesus. Jesus, who spoke of farmers and seeds and was an executed peacemaker who gave alternatives to following the economy of the violent empire, gave us communion with his body, at the Passover, broken in remembrance of him. We plant seeds and anticipate the communion bread, and we gather for the Holy Eucharist to partake in the wine and bread, grown from the land. We eat this bread as an act of peacemaking and a commitment to the good news of equal inheritance in the Beloved Community.

The abundance of God in seed production and seed saving is a model for a faithful and sacred economy. The multiplication of the economy of seed—an exponential, fragile, life-carrying agent—touches our imagination as spiritual beings. It is an economy that Jesus partook in with the multiplication of the fish and the loaves along Galilee, where a few gifts of bread and fish fed multitudes.

At Eve's Garden, our spiritual economy is one of seed saving. We save these seeds and the seeds of other heirloom vegetables from our gardens, and the return is exponential—and wrapped in indigenous wisdom. The act of seed saving ties us to generations of farmers and indigenous people from around the world. Through the economy of seed saving, we are blessed to grow even more next year. Seed saving is a seamless connector from one year to the next.

This practice of seed saving is a wonderful model for eco-justice. It is socially sound, bringing everybody together in a celebration of life and abundance. It is ecologically sound when all the seeds are poured into the same bowl and mixed around; the fields are planted the following year with very genetically diverse seeds. Certainly this seed-saving ritual is also economically redistributive. Each farmer leaves with an equal amount of seed no matter how difficult the harvest. It is an act of peacemaking, especially in this global culture, where it is anti-imperial to save your own seeds. We reverently remember the prophecies of the Lakota people, prophecies of gender equality attained through men and women gardening together.

Seed saving also connects me to the native blood within me and with the first seed savers, most of whom were women. It connects us with Vandana Shiva and the Indian seed savers who ritually gather as a community and place all their seeds into one bowl. The seeds are all mixed up and equally redistributed.

The Life-Giving Cycle Continues

The children of Camden practice and teach us communion agriculture. At Eve's Garden, the children come many days a week throughout the year, and together we work and plan our four-season harvest. One young man, eight-year-old Elijah, came to the greenhouse very regularly, always with a strong imagination and an intuitive understanding of farming. He was also very hungry when he came. Like many other children, he brought food from the greenhouse back to his family. Elijah loved to save seeds, loved to fish, and loved to grow cucumbers.

On a Saturday in early spring, Elijah came and found me in the community garden. He reached deep into his empty pockets, pulled out a tissue, and carefully unfolded it to share with me the seeds from the apple that he had eaten for breakfast. He said that he wanted to grow an apple tree so that he would never be hungry. We planted his seeds.

In June, Elijah expressed an interest in fishing. One of our neighbors brought a large duffel bag full of rods for the children on the Feast Day of St. Peter (who was also a fisherman) on June 29. On his first day of fishing, Elijah rode his bicycle down to the fishing pier in our neighborhood and brought the fish he caught back to his family and friends for frying. Later that day, Elijah knocked on my door and asked me if we could paint his fishing rod gold. He also unfolded his napkin again from his pocket and showed me the kernels that he had saved from his friend's kitchen and told me that he wanted to grow popcorn. He knew the limitless gift of the seed. We planted the seeds and painted the rod. For the rest of the summer, Elijah was either fishing or growing food for his family.

In one of the last few weeks before my eight-year-old Elijah was evicted from his house, he came to the garden and unfolded the napkin in his pocket one more time. He brought with him the gift of seed; he unfolded his napkin to reveal three acorns that he carried, which we planted to grow into oak trees. He had found these acorns in the street in front of the liquor store in our neighborhood.

I have recently been filled with much gratitude for the Jewish tradition that leaves a seat open for Elijah at the Passover seder table. During a time of drought and famine, Elijah of the Hebrew Bible prophesied that the faithfulness of God's people would bring back the rain. The Elijah I know didn't live with much wealth, and he was always hungry. But he lived in the economy of seed saving.

I also think of a lovely lady named Carmella Narducci, whom I met when I first moved to the Waterfront South neighborhood. She was an Italian woman who had moved to South Camden "straight from the boat." I remember her walking us to a street at the edge of the neighborhood called Arlington Street. This street which was once a block full of Carmella's memories and Italian genealogies, now stands as a blighted Superfund site where, of fifty-two families, only a handful were compensated after the land was poisoned. Now only two sycamore trees rise as gravestones on Arlington Street. The soil there contains thorium from the Welsbach and General Gas Mantle Company. Many of the residents of Arlington Street worked at this factory and brought home containers of the gas mantle material to their yards to be used as fill. After authorities learned of the radioactive conditions, it was at least twenty-five years before all the families moved from Arlington Street. The houses still stood, reminiscent of a blown-out Baghdad neighborhood. The consequences of war are buried in Arlington Cemetery in Washington, D.C.—and on Arlington Street in Camden.

I wrote this reflection about Arlington Street on Ash Wednesday:

> I was in the garden getting the vegetable beds ready for our St. Patrick's potato planting with a group of children from Sacred Heart School. Two of the kids hollered out from the far north side of the garden "MISS ANNNNdrea, COOoome HeEEEERe!" and I ran over to witness them hovering over a rabbit that had been recently pierced in the side and had returned to the garden to die. One of the sixth-graders decided that we should bury it, and she began to lead us in a eulogistic "Our Father ..." One of the students handed me a discarded, black, corner-store bag that had been carried there by the wind. We placed the bunny into the unbiodegradable plastic for our procession through the garden and back to the greenhouse, where we laid her to rest. As the last of the shoveled soil covered the body, one of the sixth-graders, Carlos, told us this wasn't

the only funeral he was going to this week. His cousin, who lived a few neighborhoods away, had been shot over the weekend. These children know the cycles of life and death, and our buried bunny was an act of reverence, returning to the earth for fertility and resurrection. And our story begins again …

The New Sabbath

Less Is More

UNNAMED HUNGERS

WE AS HUMAN BEINGS ARE CALLED to balance an exquisite and tumultuous array of appetites. We are programmed with an appetite to survive, with its attendant mandates to procreate, to eat, to find safe shelter, and so on. But our survival nature is not the only mandate for which we are hardwired. Empathy, generosity, and self-sacrifice serve no purpose for the needs of individual survival. Our capacity to be stunned by the beauty of a sunset or humbled by the enormity of a mountain peak does not lengthen our days or fill our bellies. Yet these, too, are human capacities— hungers, if you will—that move us to meaningful environmental action as surely as our physical hungers lead us to lunch.

Both spirit and flesh have legitimate needs and appetites, and every religion on the planet guides us in balancing these two aspects of ourselves. I don't know how the dichotomy between spirit and flesh got started, but I suspect it was a human invention. God is the author of life; our bodies and our spirits are the handiwork of the Creator. The human struggle is to integrate and balance these appetites, to satisfy both our spiritual and our physical hungers. It is imbalanced and unhealthy for us to feed one to the exclusion of the other. Yet isn't it true that, in our current era, we feed the body more than the soul?

It is true for me, and probably others, that when I am unsatisfied in spirit, I reach for comfort food. Or a vacation. Or a new sofa. I seek distractions and fullness in the physical world when I feel disquieted on the spiritual level. The mix of divine and earthly is complicated. I sense this in my own appetites. I definitely want that last slice of pizza, and yet I definitely want my guests to have enough to eat at my pizza party.

It is easier to notice and name the hungers of the body. We can actually live our whole lives without meditating, but we cannot live our lives without eating, after all. Spiritual hungers, on the other hand, are nuanced, harder to pinpoint, and easier to discount. Think about how spiritual values are dismissed in our public discourse: *airy-fairy, new agey, contemplating one's navel, a psychological crutch.* These phrases come from a corporal perspective that challenges and makes light of the spiritual. It is the more subtle, perhaps more humanizing, spiritual perspective that I wish to make obvious, to know more clearly.

I believe that we suffer tremendously—and eventually physically—when we ignore this subtle hunger. From my own experience, I know that when I fail to name and nourish the spiritual hungers, I consume in some way to distract myself from the sense of emptiness and longing. And I am no happier for it. Even more critical, if I only recognize and nourish the hungers of the flesh, my carbon footprint is going to be way bigger. Our physical appetites have a much greater impact on the physical environment.

Our spiritual hungers are intimately linked to creation; our dependence on the bounty of creation is a felt truth. Our founding prophets and teachers all had their most intimate meetings with the Eternal One in a wilderness. Each of them explicitly left the human environment to go to the artistry of the Creator. There they met God in a wind, in a small voice, in a sign or vision.

Tariq Ramadan, in *Footsteps of the Prophet,* tells us that Prophet Muhammad was raised outside the city by Bedouin family members so that his relationship with nature would function as a kind of school "where the mind gradually apprehends signs and meaning." We are urged in the Qur'an again and again to watch the seasons and the skies, for "surely there are signs in this for men of reason." The children of Israel, according to Exodus, find God's word in the sounds and sights of a storm, at the foot of a small mountain after three days of meditation. The word of God was given to them not in a library, but in an unmarked wilderness, far from the stamp of human civilization. Jesus, famously, was tested and tasked in his extended wilderness retreat.

How is it that we are so much closer to God in these "uncivilized" places?

When we live in a natural environment, the expanse of the sky is right at hand. Deep darkness follows light, and months of wintry hunger follow seasons of hunting and harvesting. But that is not the world we inhabit. It is very rare for most of us to be in an environment sculpted by the Creator. We have "conquered" nature's cycles. We can have watermelon in December if we want. We can have warmth and light all year-round. Our physical appetites are well fed. It is our hunger for awe and connection that is atrophied and redirected.

When we act, feel, and believe that we are apart from other life-forms and from our ecosystem, when we keep to the human landscape, we develop a spiritual hunger, a hunger for awe that we try to sate in many ways—even through self-stimulation and escapism as ways of seeking profound experiences—a new, less noble kind of wilderness.

The first loss is the loss of the felt connection to the fabric of life. The first loss is spiritual. After this first loss, we become interested in comforting ourselves; we somehow wish to fill the void. We look around and we see the filling of so many hungers—physical hungers—and we think, "I will fill myself with *that*!" The *that* is almost always an object. Like Adam, we begin to consume things that look appealing but are not so good for us. But our loss is real and our emptiness is real, and we really want our *that* to fill the void. And we defend our right to it with all the fear and defensiveness we feel.

Our *that* in the West is our standard of living. We have so much more than we need, and the new truth, the new connection, we are beginning to make is that this is not good for us. Truly, our enormous appetite is not good for the planet. It is not good for the skies when our intensive methods of farming and transportation clog the air with carbons. It is not good for developing countries whose local, sustainable economies are subverted by the lure of selling expensive exports to the West. And it isn't good for *us*. In addition to our original loss (spiritual), we, too, suffer in the West from the impact of climate change and political instability. Many of the wars erupting around the globe today (with their own environmental devastation) are resource wars. Without a dramatic reorientation of our economies and our consumption patterns, this can only get worse.

In our collective consciousness, one indicator of our progress as a species seems to be that we don't need to be subject to nature anymore. But we are so much the poorer for this "privilege" of rising above nature. We are robbing ourselves of our natural heritage. Of all the cancer deaths and all the environmental refugees and all the early deaths from pollution, this is another grief I find in our current situation.

It is time to rename and reclaim the subtle spiritual hungers.

Annually, the environmental justice group I direct hosts conferences where I have the delight of meeting many social pioneers who have creative insights to try to protect our environment from our audacity of trying to rise "above it." I sat in on one such class with Rev. Donna Schaper, senior minister of the Judson Memorial

Church in Manhattan. Rev. Schaper started her talk innocuously by asking folks to introduce themselves. One of us after another gave our name and said that we worked on this issue or that issue—toxins, pollution, conservation, green cleaning products, and so on. Donna smiled at the end of all that and said, "I just heard the word *work* twenty-five times. I'm tired out from this introduction."

She proceeded to share an awesome lecture with us about the Sabbath. She spoke about a hunger for life that can become greed, a hunger for more. We might want so much of life that we actually ignore our own need for rest. We need to disconnect, not from life but from the constant chain of acquiring and achieving. To quote another teacher, Rabbi Arthur Waskow, we risk becoming human-doings instead of human-beings. Donna spoke about the necessity to stop, reflect, and realign ourselves, for our own long-term safety and well-being. I asked her to share the power of the idea behind her concept of "Green Sabbath"—and our resistance to it.

Green Sabbath
BY REV. DONNA SCHAPER, PhD
Senior Minister, Judson Memorial Church, New York City

Green means sustainable living on earth. It's not just a color but a complex of behaviors that turns us into humans, and earth into Earth. *Green* is more about less: We don't do things so much as refrain from doing them. *Lessness* is its objective. One holiday, my eldest convinced me of the entire meaning of lessness being more-ness. I was about to weary myself making yet one more casserole (someone's "old" favorite). We already had nine dishes on the table. He said, with a hand on my sagging, unsabbathed shoulder, "Mom, less is more." We didn't need the casserole.

Sabbath means sustainable living on earth. It's not just a ritual but a complex of behaviors as well. It refrains from action at certain moments so that reflection can enhance action at a later point. This last sentence is more instrumental than necessary. Sabbath is not a *way to enhance* action so much as a behavior that *does enhance* action by dethroning it from its 24/7 roost and reign on our lives. We don't practice Sabbath as a way to get more. We practice Sabbath as a way to do and be less.

By *Green Sabbath* I mean a custom-designed day that we can practice while the world comes to its senses. It is a necessary vision of a common quiet. I experienced a taste of this heaven once in Israel, when on a Saturday we were just walking along without accompaniment of noise, cars, or commerce. There were five of us in this little group. It was exhilarating to move in time and space without simultaneous hyperactivity. Do I know how much different religionists like to fight about the right way to do Sabbath? Yes. Do I think the world will ever agree on a right way? No. So why suggest some unrealistic idea like a Green Sabbath, a common quiet? Because the world is desperate for it. Realistically, if people don't get some downtime and some quiet, the world will explode with anxiety. We won't need bombs. We'll explode from the unnourished inside out.

Green Sabbath is an idea that pushes buttons on an economic, political, religious, and personal level all at once. It refrains from purchasing things at certain times. It creates a politically savvy instead of politically stupid populace. Religiously, it links us to ancient people who appear not to have been as backward as our idolatrous modernity thinks. Personally, it disciplines us for the practice of the presence of God.

People can Sabbath the "Jewish way" or the "Christian way" or the "Muslim way" or their own way. All are good ways. As I pointed out in my book *Sabbath Keeping,* modernity has so broken our folk patterns that we probably have to find our own method of keeping a Sabbath. We probably don't know how to do it in the way of our forebears or our faiths. And if we did know how "they" used to do it, we may find our own family schedules (soccer on the Sabbath?) or our own work schedules (catching up on e-mail on Sunday?) to be prohibitive of the old way. Christians used to eat a pot roast on Sundays with the extended family, and then rest and talk in the living room. Or so they did in my family of origin. Try to find the family now! Or cook the pot roast among all the vegans! The old ways are not wrong so much as inconvenient. Sabbath is an *inconvenient truth*. But when it goes beyond inconvenience to impossible, new ways need to be imagined.

As a first step toward lessness, can we practice three quiet hours on one day a week that we designate as "our" Sabbath? Muslims hold a spiritual gathering day on Friday, Jews on Saturday, Christians on Sunday. That gives us a three-day window for an ecumenical Sabbath. In Morocco, I realized that I had to do my shopping Monday through Thursday because all three faiths had Shabbat on one of the weekend days. You never knew what would be open. Think Siesta Sabbath. Think about a French lunch. Think about ways that don't hurt commerce (because religion has lost the battle against commerce), and let stores and businesses be open in a way that allows us to prepare for the impending quietude. But in the three-hour flextime Sabbath, imagine the quiet. Imagine the prayer that is possible. Many people can't get to my congregation on Sundays. Or to yours on Fridays or Saturdays. Make it easier to worship. Open the synagogues and the mosques and the churches on a flextime schedule. Or practice Sabbath in nature or in solitude. And again, just imagine the quiet. Imagine the freedom. Imagine the reflection. Go ahead, let yourself be utopian. That is what Sabbath keeping does to people. It helps us refuse to put up with constant stress as a form of life.

I was just with an old friend's ninety-four-year-old mother. Word was out that she was breathing her last breath, and I rushed to the hospital. When I got there, I saw a fully intubated woman moving her head back and forth in nervous distress. The doctor was there and remembered the "pad" trick. The woman could at least write. So he got her a pad, and she scrawled weakly on it, "Water." He said to her, "Anita, do you want something to drink? Are you thirsty?" Instead of getting what we thought we would get, which was a pathetic but certain yes, we got an angry shake of the head NO.

Back to the paper. When I returned the paper to her, she scrawled on it with even greater effort, "Water the plants." She was not ready to die. She was still caring about something outside herself. And here we were having the disconnect-Mom-from-life-support conversation in the waiting room! How wrong we would have been. Having said that, and hoping the reader appreciates the humor of my mother's friend, permit me to move on to my real subject.

During Sabbath keeping, it is not that you *water* the plants, but that you *receive* the water. For Green Sabbath to work, we need the permission to receive water.

Many of us will have to practice receiving water. Thus, my recommendation to start small and stay small in a modified three-hour version of practicing the practice of the presence of God. Think reps in a gym: First you lift five pounds eight times, then you lift the same five pounds twelve times, then you increase your capacity to lift weights. To practice the Sabbath of *not* lifting anything, we need just as much practice. Before we could even imagine a world of a one-day Sabbath again—not to mention such a matter in an increasingly multifaith world—we would have to know how to do a little bit of it at a time.

In my recommendation of a Green Sabbath, first custom-designed, then democratically implemented at wider and wider levels, I want you to be the plant, not the waterer. I want you to be the fig tree, not the gardener. I want you to be a part of the world and its earth, not in charge of it. Yes, this Green Sabbath is all about selfishness. It is pro-selfishness. It is about clearing the haze that comes from moralism on behalf of the clarity that comes from sustainable selves. Many of us are just plain foggy most of the time. We don't know what is really important, so we try to do everything. Selfishness clears the haze; it says, "Know who you are and take good care of who you are."

My advocacy of selfishness, of taking care of ourselves first, is spiritual first, then practical. I'll start with the spiritual. Who did my deathbed friend think she was? She thought she was who she has been for ninety-four years, a matriarch (I think she was born that way), the last samurai of the "save the world set" over lunch. Yes, she ran a UN women's group. Why bother with the local garden club when there was a whole world to consider? She had delusions of grandeur, which a little cancer and pneumonia did not stop. She was a giver, not a receiver. With her last bit of strength, she was worried about the plants! To call her imperialist or idolatrous would be unfair, but to note that even under conditions when a little giving back to her might have been warranted, she could not rest or receive. When we only give and don't receive, only fruit and never fallow, only imagine ourselves as the gardener and never as the tree, we stand comfortably on the threshold of both idolatry and imperialism. These are forms of spiritual impoverishment, not wealth.

From these idolatrous places, we get tired. We just get tired. We get tired of hearing about how warm winters have upset the rhythms of maple sugar. Instead of getting sapped, we *are* sapped. You know what I mean. There sits global warming. We should, we *must,* do something about it, but what might we do? We are tapped out of ideas and sapped of spiritual strength.

Thus I am changing my approach. I have long known that we live with contradictory biblical commandments. Are we to save or savor the world? I think the answer is both, and that the way we do both is by doing less of both. Let me explain.

Before we save the world, we must remember to savor it. Before we empty on behalf of another, we should fill ourselves up.

Selfishness is willing to nourish others but wants to think about it first. Selfishness sees that prophetic action—anything that saves any little part of the world—comes from the overflow of our full fountain. It is "my cup runneth over time," not "my cup empties out." We do need to care for the world, but we can care for it from nourishment, not hunger or thirst. We ourselves are plants rooted here by the Creator. We are not the Gardener; we are not God. We can grow a few figs, each of us, and that's it. Trying to be more, or to imagine that we are more, can produce "colony-collapse disorder." This relatively recent and alarming phenomenon among bee colonies results in the sudden death of hives, and preliminary studies show that there is at least some significant possibility that the phenomenon is correlated to poor nutrition and "extraordinary stress." We need to pay attention to nature's lesson.

Whenever we overgarden, and over*role* ourselves as gardeners, we forget that we are trees. Just trees. Wow. What a great thing to be a fruiting tree! There is no shame in being a tree. There is no minimum requirement for production. A tree in its first three years is protected in Leviticus (19:23–25). It is granted the time it needs to mature and become a stable source before it is pressed into the service of an orchard. How dare anyone judge us as useless because we haven't fruited for three years?

Spiritually, we replace trust and grace for arrogance and hyperactivity. Sounds good to me. Practically, we do less—but we do less *intentionally*. And by that intentionality, we do more. We work on fruiting a little bit, not a lot. We get hold of the fog and haze of commandments and bring them to clarity about our fruiting. That task alone is fertilizer for most people today. We can come out of the fog of thinking that we need to do everything that everybody wants us to do and, in the clarity, see who and where we are.

Rip Van Winkle is us. After a long sleep, we are just waking up in the twenty-first century. It may be that we human beings need to reinterpret ourselves before anything will be done about global warming. We need to reexamine this notion of ourselves as the responsible agents, that we are those who water the plants, not those who need water. Our lives may need to look more like the lives of people in developed countries: cooperators with nature, not her master. A Green Sabbath is our practice of resting in nature, not controlling her. Green Sabbath is a personal spiritual practice that has prophetic impact. Its secret is doing less on behalf of more.

CREATING NEW SABBATH RITUALS

Since hearing Donna's talk, I have decided to be an activist and a *relaxivist*. You can quote me on that and add the word to your spell-checker. It's an idea that I hope will get around. It's not easy! Our activity has an addictive quality. We are identified with our work. Pausing gives us time to ponder ... what? What is it in our lives that we do not contemplate as we skate from one thing to another? Whatever that is, it *will* surface on a Sabbath. We will have made time for it, and we will now be in relationship to it. We will notice it, like the sound of a dripping faucet that is suddenly deafening when the vacuum cleaner is turned off.

Many of my Jewish friends have a kind of Buddhist-envy because Buddhists have such a helpful system of meditation for quieting our interior "noise." Many folks today are drawn to that. We seem to sense that we are missing something. The Dalai Lama has lived through horrendous suffering and abuse, but he finds it hard to be in the United States for long periods. He finds us disquieting. If we reclaimed and practiced Sabbath, the Buddhists would have nothing on us!

Sabbath, however, as it is said, is not natural. There is nothing particularly natural about the number seven, and there is nothing in nature (save a mythological river named Sambatyon) that stops for a day. And yet all life on earth rests. We rest in the winter, we rest at night. Our hearts beat and pause, beat and pause, as long as we are alive. From the first words of the First Testament, we are offered—actually required to have—this gift of a day of pause and reflection: "Remember the Sabbath day, and keep it holy. Six days you shall labor and do all your work. But the seventh day is a Sabbath to the Lord your God; you shall not do any work" (Exodus 20:8–10a, NRSV).

Can we create new ways of observing Sabbath that would allow us to reclaim ourselves, reclaim our time? Can we create Sabbath rituals that would feed our spiritual hungers by reconnecting with the cycles and seasons of life? If we could rebalance the appetites of our bodies with the appetites of our spirit, we would need less "stuff" to satisfy our needs. If we could learn to honor and ritualize the unique patterns in a day, a year, a life, we—and our planet—would be the richer for it.

Through the years, I have had the good fortune to work with some amazing reclaimers of a deeper sense of spiritual heritage. One such person is an educator in Connecticut named David Blumenkranz. David was trained in youth services and had come to the conclusion that we were not offering our kids real and meaningful challenges to test themselves in their transition from childhood to adulthood. He made a cross-cultural study of rites of passage and began to incorporate them into his work. David and I teamed up for a few years and offered Rites of Passage Experiences (ROPE retreats) based on his studies. We took one seventh-grade class on a weekend retreat that involved an overnight meditation "at a place in the woods, a place of your choosing—which has been waiting for you since the time of creation," according to David's instructions to the youth. The adolescents were sent out "to find their place" in the woods, accompanied by a piece of paper containing a few verses from the Torah reading that was to be read at their bar or bat mitzvah in the coming year.

On Sunday morning, the adults, including the kids' parents, built a fire outside at the edge of the woods. We began to sing a song together from Psalms, a chant really, asking for guidance at this new step in our lives and in our children's lives. The children had been instructed not to return to the camp until they heard us. So we adults had to pray loud and strong for our voices to reach all the young people. When they heard our strong voices calling for guidance, they began to stream back to the fire pit. We adults had formed a circle around the fire and each of the young people traveled that circle, being welcomed into the community—as the new people they were—by each and every one of us. That weekend was so memorable that I have trouble describing it without crying.

A ritual should be that strong and meaningful, especially for the transition from childhood to adulthood, which involves a loss—a death of one stage and the emergence of another. We need guidance and community and support to really make these kinds of transitions. Every one of the kids on that retreat stayed active in their Hebrew school until they left for college. They were mentors and tutors to the younger kids. All of them kept the pictures of the place of their private forest retreat. David's ritual also made the adults form a stronger community, and that had a lasting effect as well.

This simple heritage of community and meaningful transitions has slipped away from us. We tend to gravitate to rituals haphazardly, if at all, when life transitions approach or events seem overwhelming. But daily and weekly rituals of resting and quieting are just as important. The very cycles and seasons of life are tuned to the hum of the dance of our planet in the cosmos. If we plant our rituals squarely in this greater life, they will hold the meaning they are meant to have, and we will find comfort and support from the Author of Life.

Aren't our religious traditions meant to help us in this way? So how can we reclaim that?

Sabbath is practiced, most often, in community. As we make time to notice our subtler perceptions together, we will have the support and inspiration of a community. Time and consciousness will take on a more spacious quality. Our bodies will relax. We will smile more. We will be fed in a different way. The rabbis say that Sabbath brings us an extra soul. We can come back to our very important work with more capacity and compassion. Sabbath allows us to taste the kind of wealth, the spiritual wealth, that we wish to multiply in the world. Sabbath opens our eyes to the subtle gifts, to the reality that "Less is more." Sabbath moves us into a less consuming and more caretaking mode for the earth.

However, Sabbath will not get into the world by our talking about it. It's a subtle thing that will emanate from us only when we drink of it. When we find a way to give *and* receive, we will be more balanced beings. When we trust enough to rest and receive rather than to constantly do and act and make, we will be quieter beings with a smaller carbon footprint. When we honor the needs of the body and the needs of the spirit, we will be truer to ourselves and better neighbors to the other life-forms with which we share this planet.

8

Eco-Conversion

A New Paradigm for a New Earth

SEEING WITH GREEN EYES

ENVIRONMENTAL CONSCIOUSNESS IS NOT JUST A GREEN PATCH on our religious belief system; questions about our role in creation are core to every faith tradition. Our deepest religious paradigms must address these questions. Although the extent of our impact on the systems of earth is new, our religious ideals are enduring. Perhaps we are asking new questions of our faiths. Perhaps we are looking with "green eyes" at our teachings. But surely our Eternal God and our great teachers have guidance for us here.

I think of the time I met a new environmental justice colleague on the telephone. From her name, she could have been Jewish, and I wanted to find out whether that was so. I dropped a short Yiddish word into the conversation to see whether she found it familiar.

"What did you say?" she asked.

"*Shabbos,*" I replied, "Yiddish for Sabbath." And I proceeded to tell her that traditional Jews all around the world live within a mile or two from the synagogue so they can walk to services, because none of them will drive on the Sabbath.

She was fascinated. "That means they live near each other, too!" she astutely observed.

"Sure," I replied, starting to catch her excitement.

"My gosh," she mused, "if I told my ecology friends that there is a community of people in most of the major cities of the world who live near each other so they can share meals and holidays and so much else … I think they would have trouble believing it!"

I suddenly saw for the first time that a commitment to not driving on the Sabbath would mean just that: People would be able to help each other with child care, visit on weekends, share meals frequently—all without driving. Of the many Jewish people who refrain from driving on Sabbath, I think only a small percentage of them view it as an environmental mandate, and yet that, too, is the obvious result.

I began to consider what other teachings and practices of our faith tradition could be seen in this green light. This work of seeing anew what is in our traditions is an effort I now share with other faith-based activists. I learned that a cherished colleague, Rev. Margaret Bullitt-Jonas, was engaged in a study of the theology of Christianity as a paradigm for her own ecological passion. Rev. Margaret, an Episcopal priest and a ferocious earth steward, who serves on the Leadership Council of Religious Witness for the Earth, feels that her tradition addresses our ecological crisis at this juncture, and she finds tremendous solace and power in her Christianity. Her life work brings together her journey as a Christian and her focus on care of creation in a kind of honest struggle that is religious witnessing at its best, and I think many will find Margaret's words valuable, whatever their faith of origin.

Conversion to Eco-Justice
BY REV. MARGARET BULLITT-JONAS, PhD
Leadership Council of Religious Witness for the Earth, Littleton, Massachusetts

Every year, countless congregations across the country celebrate Earth Day by setting aside a Sunday to focus on God's creation.

The truth is, I haven't always been a big fan of Earth Day. I used to think of Earth Day as being kind of retro—a quaint throwback to the time when I was young and foolish and wore tie-dyed shirts and bell-bottoms. I used to think that Earth Day was for tree huggers, for people who liked tinkering with solar-powered contraptions, or for people who dreamed of living on a farm. Surely we had outgrown all that, I would tell myself—we who had entered the modern, electronic age in which most of us live in cities and are too busy and stressed out raising families and working long hours to waste time on secondary things. Earth Day was for sentimental types. I had better things to do.

Today I look back on my supposedly sophisticated point of view as completely naïve. The environmental crisis has made me acutely aware of our dependence on clean air and healthy soil, and our interdependence with all living beings. There is nothing sentimental about being alarmed that fully a quarter of the world's animal and plant species may be driven into extinction just a few decades from now. There is nothing sentimental about being upset that so many kids in inner cities now suffer from asthma caused by air pollution. There is nothing sentimental about being shocked that the rise of only a single degree in average worldwide temperatures—when a much greater rise is forecast in the years ahead—is already heating the deep oceans, melting glaciers, causing lethal floods and droughts, and changing patterns of bird migration.

In the Gospel of John, the risen Christ appears on the seashore and asks a poignant question as he watches his troubled disciples try in vain to catch some fish: "Children, you have no fish, have you?" (John 20:5, NRSV). Jesus might as well be posing the question to us, for often enough we, too, do not have fish. The United States Commission on Ocean Policy reports that pollution, overfishing, and poor management are jeopardizing the health of North America's oceans. Too often the fish we do have are contaminated with toxic chemicals, such as PCP or mercury. And it is not just fish stocks that are being rapidly depleted; researchers warn that human beings are gobbling up the world's natural resources so fast that, if current population trends and rates of exploitation continue, by the year 2050 we will need two earths to cope with the demand.

No, it is not sentimentality that leads us to honor Earth Day and to care about the fate of the planet; it is hardheaded realism. We have no future if we poison, deplete, and destroy the very ecosystem on which our life depends.

The questions that I have been wrestling with for several years are these: What needs to happen inside us in order for us to place care for the earth at the center of our moral and spiritual concern? What deep change in perspective, what significant shift in values, must we experience before we become willing to offer ourselves to the great work of healing the earth? Such a conversion makes a person like me turn from pooh-poohing Earth Day to cherishing it as a day to lift up our conviction that God loves the world that God made, and that God calls us to be partners in the work of environmental justice and healing. Our conversion to eco-justice may or may not be as dramatic as what the Apostle Paul experienced on the road to Damascus. Unlike Paul's conversion, ours may involve no flash of lightning, no voice from the heavens, no falling helplessly to the ground, no sudden onset of blindness. But our conversion to eco-justice can certainly go as deep, challenging us to a radical reorientation of our lives.

For Christians, eco-conversion often involves three steps or stages: creation, crucifixion, and resurrection.

The Creation Stage

The first stage, *creation*, is when we fall in love with the beauty of God's creation. We experience amazement, gratefulness, wonder, and awe. In this first stage of the journey, we discover how loved we are as creatures made in the image of God and connected by breath, blood, bone, and flesh to the whole of God's creation.

I do not take this first step for granted. It is a huge discovery to experience creation as sacred. I, for one, grew up in a city, and to some degree we city dwellers are cut off from the natural world. We cannot see the stars at night; we cannot hear the spring peepers. Here in Boston our water may come from a source a hundred miles distant, and our food from places six thousand or seven thousand miles away. *Nature* can become an abstraction, nothing more than the weather that does or does not get in my way as I hurry into my car and drive from one building to the next.

What's more, many of us—as I did—grew up in a family riddled with addiction. Or we developed an addiction of our own. If you have ever been close to an addict, you know that addiction functions to disconnect us from the needs and rhythms of the body. In my own years of addiction, I paid no attention to my body's signals. I not only ignored my body, I openly defied it. It did not matter whether I was tired, sad or angry, lonely or anxious; whatever I was feeling, I stuffed it down with food. One night I had a dream that even the squirrels hated me. It was a telling dream, not only because it reflected the addict's self-hatred, but also because it reflected the addict's deep disconnection from the natural world. The more thoroughly we cut ourselves off from our bodies, from nature, from our embodied humanity, the more we also cut ourselves off from God.

I began my recovery in 1982, and in the years that followed, I gradually learned to honor the first bit of nature with which I had been entrusted: my own body. As I learned to listen to my body and to live within its limits, I also began to connect with nature. I began to see that God loved not only my body, but also the whole "body" of creation. My prayer began to change. It was like turning my pocket inside out; whereas once I'd found God mostly in silent, inward contemplation, now God began showing up around me—in the pond, the rocks, the willow tree. If you spend an hour gazing at a willow tree, after a while it begins to disclose itself and to disclose

God. I began to understand the words of poet Gerard Manley Hopkins: "The world is charged with the grandeur of God." I began to understand the words of Genesis: "God saw everything that [God] had made, and indeed, it was very good" (Genesis 1:31, NRSV).

Creation is the stage when we discover the great love affair that is going on between God and God's world. We enter that stage when we experience God's love for us, and not only for us, not only for our own kind. Because God's love is infinite, this stage is one that we can never outgrow and never finish exploring.

The Crucifixion Stage

The second stage is *crucifixion*. Nobody likes this part of the journey, but it is becoming harder and harder to avoid. The more fully we experience the ways in which the creation reveals the love of God, the more we cannot help seeing and sensing the relentless assault on the natural world: clear-cut forests, extinct species, vanishing topsoil, ocean "dead zones," disappearing wetlands, acid rain, an increasingly hot and unstable climate.

We try not to notice these things. We try to shrug them off or look away. But crucifixion is the place where God finally breaks through our denial. When we reach this stage, we finally dare to feel the pain, to mourn what we have lost and what our children will never see. It is important to feel our protest and grief because it is an expression of our love. We cannot sidestep this stage if we are to become truly human. I wonder what the church would be like if it became a genuine sanctuary, a place where we felt free to mourn, free to express our anger and sorrow about what is happening to the earth.

When Christians come to the foot of the cross, we express not only our grief, but also our guilt, because if we are honest with ourselves, we must confess the ways that we ourselves benefit from the destruction of the earth. We must admit our own patterns of consumption and waste. When it comes to eco-justice, none of us—at least, not most North Americans—can stand in a place of self-righteousness, because we, too, are implicated.

After Paul's dramatic conversion, he spent three days in blindness, eating and drinking nothing. I wonder if Paul did not weep with penitence and sorrow during those three days of fasting when he could see nothing but the darkness of what he had done. He had reached his own inner cross, the place of self-awareness where God gives us grace to face our malice, ignorance, grief, and guilt. It is at the cross that evil and suffering are continually met by the love of God, and in a time of ecological crisis, we may need to take hold of the cross as never before.

The Resurrection Stage

In the first stage of eco-conversion, we let ourselves fall in love with the beauty of God's world. In the second stage, we share in Christ's crucifixion, letting ourselves mourn creation's wounds and acknowledge our own deep grief and guilt. And in the third stage, we gradually come to share in Christ's *resurrection*. Filled with the love that radiates through all creation, and empowered by the cross that, like a lightning rod, grounds all suffering and sin in the love of God, we come at last to bear witness to the Christ "who bursts out of the tomb, who proclaims that life, not death, has the last word, and who gives us power to roll away the stone."* When we are led to resurrection, we move out into the world to participate in works of caring for creation. A sure sign of having entered this stage is when, through the power of the risen Christ, we become seekers of justice and agents of healing.

---

*This quotation is from "To Serve Christ in All Creation—A Pastoral Letter from the Episcopal Bishops of New England," sent to the Episcopal Churches of Province One on the Feast of the Presentation of Christ, 2003.

Our action can take many forms. God's creation needs healing at every level, so wherever we feel prompted to begin is a good place to start. Commitment to care for the earth will affect what we buy and what we refuse to buy, what we drive and what we refuse to drive, how we heat our homes, how much we reuse and recycle, whether we are willing to do something as simple as switch to compact fluorescent light bulbs, whether—and for whom—we vote, and whether we go even further and engage in public protest and civil disobedience.

The resurrected life is no solo affair. Paul needed someone—a man named Ananias—to help him make sense of what he had experienced and to heal his blindness, and Paul in turn created small communities as he made his way around the Mediterranean, bearing witness to Christ. The resurrected life is a life lived in community, filled with hope and fired by love. In the work of environmental care and justice, we need to find allies and to join a network so our actions will be strategic and effective.

Left to our own devices, it is easy to feel paralyzed and overwhelmed because there is so much to do. Conversely, we can run around doing everything at once but be ineffective, and burn out before we have accomplished a thing. As my brother-in-law wryly observes, "Don't haul water in a bucket full of holes."

Many Americans do mark Earth Day, but you know as well as I do that a lot of us want to ignore the environmental crisis, to deny its urgency, to deal with it some other time. I read somewhere that comedian George Carlin once remarked, "I don't believe there's any problem in this country, no matter how tough it is, that Americans, when they roll up their sleeves, can't completely ignore."

When we Americans get past our denial and actually take a look at the challenges we face, what may come next *is* despair—the awful sense that it is too late, that it has gone too far, that we will not be able to turn this around. I know of only two antidotes to despair: prayer and action. Prayer roots us in the first stage of that three-part journey—namely, in the love of God that extends through all creation. Prayer also gives us courage to enter the second stage, as we share Christ's crucifixion, mourn the losses, and feel the grief. And through the Spirit of the risen Christ, we embark on the third stage: we are sent out to act, to do what we can to transform the world.

There is good nourishment to be had in a life lived like that. When, in the Gospel of John, the risen Christ appears on the seashore and tells the exhausted disciples where to cast their nets, the depleted fishery is restored, the disciples are refreshed, and the risen Christ himself prepares and serves them a meal. The bread and fish that he gives them are a sign of God's abundance; they recall the multiplication of loaves and fishes, when everyone on the hillside sat down and was fed.

When Christians come to the communion table and share the blessed bread and wine, we, too, are fed; we, too, taste the marvelous generosity of the God who loved us—and all creation—into being. Eco-conversion invites us to become people of prayer, people who take time to steep ourselves in the love of God. And it invites us to become people of action, too, people who try in every aspect of our lives—from what we eat to what we drive and how we vote—to move toward ecological sanity and sustainability, and to honor our first and most basic God-given call: to become caregivers of the earth.

THE POWER OF WITNESSING

Eco-conversion. What a lovely word. I have seen it at work again and again. I think of Carol, a Jewish friend who was struggling financially because her husband had been laid off. Their financial commitments (kids in sports and art lessons, minivan) were so extensive that they were cutting back on food and had stopped inviting their friends over for Sabbath meals. (If you saw the price of kosher meat, you would understand this very well.) Over the course of a long conversation, Carol decided that a family with two teenage girls needs friends and a community more than they need a minivan. And she eventually agreed that her friends might come for a meal, even if the food was a pot of hearty soup and a loaf of bread.

The ranks of the environmental activists are filled with unlikely candidates who had perfectly normal lives and then developed abnormal rashes or lost a pet to pesticides applied on their lawns or developed breast cancer. This personal loss hit them with all the force of the tragedy it was. And then they noticed that they were not alone. They did not get cancer because of some personal failing. They did not lose their pet because of some fault of their own. They experienced these losses because we are all exposed to a sea of toxic chemicals in the course of modern life. And so their eco-conversion begins.

Others of us feel the first compelling urge to eco-conversion because of a loss of something wondrous, as my friend Lynn Fulkerson witnesses:

> When I was five, I moved to "the country" where my parents built a house on property that had been a chicken farm. Behind our house were cornfields and beyond lay woods, where I spent most of my early childhood. I discovered that the woods were full of miracles, and I was filled with wonder. Those were the days when parents could let their children run free. Carpools and youth sports had not been invented yet, and my imagination was allowed to run wild in those woods. I can say that it was my first real love affair.

My friends and I had a secret place, of course. There a small brook coursed through mossy banks that were covered with violets and trillium, jack-in-the-pulpit, and ferns. We called it "Paradise," and as we stepped off the school bus, we called to one another, "Meet you in Paradise!"

On a visit home from college, my father told me about a new housing development in the neighborhood. I recall racing out the door, through the backyards that were the cornfields, and toward the woods, which had grown up into giant colonials, up the newly paved streets to find Paradise Lost. All that was left of the creek was what ran through a concrete pipe.

That was the moment for me. I was a convert, transformed by grief. In my fifties and studying at Hartford Seminary, I discovered a connection between my faith and my love for the planet. How could I have been so blind as not to see and not to hear the call in our scripture and in my tradition, in the hymns and psalms we sing, to love all of God's creation?

Lynn experienced something that changed her, and she became a force for change in her denomination, and in her town and in her state. She observed her own experiences, her own sense of loss and mandate, and she shared from her heart with others.

This kind of witnessing plays a role in the three Abrahamic faiths. In each case, it means to give testimony about what you understand to be true. It is an expression of and support for the faithful, even though—and perhaps because—some of these truths are subtle and hard to put into words. There is an effort to find a shared language of experience that helps others on the journey. In Lynn's case, she did not splice her environmentalism onto her Episcopalian faith; she experienced them as one and the same. Her experience had the force of a convergence and a conversion, a power that spurred her to take action and assume leadership.

In the case of Eboo Patel, founding director of the Interfaith Youth Core, his witness is helping to bring about surprising partnerships between Muslims and evangelicals on college campuses among students who want to care for creation. He speaks freely and frequently about his Muslim values to care for the beauty and diversity of creation. He remembers hearing as a child that Adam, the first man, representative of all humanity, was the *A'BD* and *khalifa,* the servant and representative, of God on earth. After he read Rachel Carson's dark prophecy of environmental collapse in her book *Silent Spring,* he returned to those verses, and the phrase struck him in a new way: "This commandment, to be a steward of earth, is cosmic, concrete, and collective. This is a universal story that Muslims should reconnect with and share with others." In Patel's organization, evangelicals and Muslims often work together in organizing practical environmental stewardship projects. An Interfaith Day of Service in 2008 was held in fifty cities around the world, and many of their youth chose environmental projects as their project. This one person's witness nourishes a multitude of communities' eco-activism.

As people of faith, we can support each other to move from numbness and despair toward hope and renewal by sharing our stories, making our witness known. We can value creation as sacred. We can acknowledge and express our sadness and remorse. We can be ready to move out into the world with action, with the support of prayer and community.

In the Jewish tradition, these are the steps of *teshuvah,* repentance or return. We return to our original holy nature, we feel remorse for the environmental degradation we have caused, and we resolve to do differently going forward. Even when we have an opportunity to despoil and waste, we resist. We act in accordance with our resolve.

GOING FORWARD

I hope I have made eco-converts out of you, or at least have supported and nourished your own commitment to earth stewardship. It would be tempting, and perhaps even a welcome end to the book, to conclude with a list of things you can do to save the planet. But these lists already exist (some appear in the Appendices), and they are not the parting words of this book.

The thought I want to leave you with is this: *The environmental crisis is the manifestation of a spiritual problem.* The overconsumption, waste, and greed that imperil us are the reflection of our inability to enjoy the real pleasures and the real challenges of the human condition. What we must do cannot be reduced to a list of safer cosmetics and cleansers to buy—though that is surely useful. What I advise is more of a process and a journey, which will not fit so well in a list.

I hope to be part of an effort of waking up, to reclaim and reframe the delight of being human. I would like to reclaim my frailness as a mortal human being who is part of nature and not above her. I would like to reclaim the park near my house and the sky and the seasons and the cosmos as my home. I would like to feel at peace and at rest—often—as a resident in this home.

I wish to deepen the connections with my neighbors (and who is *not* my neighbor on this tiny planet?). I hope that our meaningful work together (and play together and meals together) will continue to be truly nourishing.

I hope to know and internalize the simple fact that being on a budget is not shameful; it is not a sign of inadequacy or a form of child abuse. Living within our limits—our energetic, financial, and environmental limits—is truth, not failure. It is not patriotic to waste. It is not a sign of success to overconsume. It is a sign of success to know ourselves, to know what we need and what we want, and to share that authentic knowledge with others.

Ours is a spiritual crisis. This is where the healing lies.

Limitations are our teachers. They give us an opportunity to be clear, to be strong, and to be realistic. The natural limitations reflected in the environmental challenge are a form of feedback from the universe. We'd best read this book of nature and take its lessons to heart.

As we internalize this new context, our next step of empowerment is to join with others. In our churches, mosques, and synagogues. In our town halls and places of work. In our neighborhoods. It is fine if our gatherings are small. It is fine if we take small steps together, as long as these steps are based on real needs, real hopes, and a real communion of spirit. The power of this kind of action spreads in a way that is different from that of an international commission or an editorial in a large newspaper.

There are many ways to be influential. Powerful, well-calibrated healing efforts spread like the scent of lilacs on the wind. Others will follow your lead or implement your model or be inspired by your project. Even if they never even hear of your work, they will be supported by it nonetheless. You will be saying no to fantasies and false hungers, and you will be saying yes to love and connection and spirit. Your steps will rebalance the whole; we are all in this together.

Some of you will garden. Some of you will set more realistic family budgets and support each other in the transitions. Some of you will start small businesses to carry the green revolution into the mainstream economy. Some of you will bike more. Some of you will work together to make your homes more efficient. And some of you will create strategies that I cannot begin to imagine because *your* truth will lead you to new places that no one has imagined yet because we are in the image of our Creator, and our God is an abundantly creative maker.

I am inspired in this by the way in which crystals form. When the ingredients that can form into crystals float in a solution, they look like nothing more than mud. Two things are required for them to "drop out" of solution and form, magically, wholly, suddenly into crystals of stunning beauty. First, the dissolved, precrystalline material must come into contact with a formed, if minute, crystal, sometimes called a "seed crystal." Their bond must be stronger than the natural forces that would break them apart, the flotsam and water currents around the newly formed bonds. Second, there must be a change in climate (!), such as temperature, pressure, or pH balance. That natural pressure will force the crystalline material to bond together in sudden beauty where before only mud was visible.

I believe that the purity of our hearts, as we pray for and work toward our own preservation and the defense of the natural order, creates in us the minute crystal form, the seed. That form then attracts others who are destined, together, to shape the transformation. We are the crystal seeds and our partnerships are the bonds. Our sincere intentions and our inner work are the beauty of the form we will create together.

In the end, I come back to my firm belief that religion can save the environment. We are commanded to it. Our dedication to the garden is our first vocation. We have the passion and the influence to do it. We have the vision and numbers and persistence necessary. We have the spiritual tools to meet the spiritual aspect of the challenge. And we have the spiritual tools to nurture ourselves and others during the losses that are already under way.

Who among us has not buried a loved one because of the environmental epidemics rampant among us? Humans are a so-called indicator species; our health and well-being are indicators of the health of the ecosystem. And we are not well. Great courage is required to see these illnesses as an epidemic, not just a personal tragedy. In support of each other, we can muster the strength to see this—just to *see* it. It is an enormous thing to take in. This knowledge becomes our mandate to undertake the journey of change. But we will need each other and our faith and our hope for a different course—just to see what is true.

And the environment can save religion. This project of living our oneness is urgent. We will need to see our way clearly to remove every obstacle from the path of this mandate. Every prejudice and historical hatred will need to be wiped away. Every religious principle that is espoused but not embodied must be shaken out and reinvigorated. When we steal and burn and bomb and massacre each other, we are destroying the shared heritage of our earth and denigrating the divine image. Every destructive act is a threat to the very self-preservation we espouse. Environmentalism can save religion by giving us a living laboratory in which we can learn to live up to our religion's aspirations.

Years ago, I quit smoking, not because my kids begged me to, so that I would live to see my grandchildren, but because I coughed up tar-stained mucus. I was afraid for my life. From the very first story of Adam and Eve, we humans seem to learn more through dreaded consequences than through inspiration. If we mark the environmental consequences already among us, we will be well motivated to change. If we name the pain—the spiritual pain and the physical imbalances—we will be well on our way to change.

There is a line in the Jewish Sabbath liturgy that says that God does not grant grace and satiety and serenity to people who are thick or misguided or alienated. I have always read that line with some discomfort because it seems punitive. But I have recently understood that it is not God who withholds grace. It is not that God refuses to rest in those who are astray. The spirit cannot rest in us unless we rest in it, unless we make quiet times in our days and quiet places in our hearts and minds. We cannot have this ease unless we make room for it.

Of the many ways we—all of us—name God, my favorite is a Hebrew name that contains the Hebrew letter *hey*, twice. *Hey*, which makes the sound of the English *h,* is the sound of an open throat, and there are two of them in this name of God. This is said to be the ineffable name of God. It is unpronounceable. It is the sound of a breath. I love the idea that the name of God is the breath going in and out of the lungs of living things.

Where will we find our center, our power, our source in this vast environmental effort? In a still, small voice, said Jesus. In all things, says the Qur'an. In the breath of your nostrils, said King David.

Perhaps the best way to end this book—and to begin the environmental witness to which we are called—is to conclude with a prayer from the Psalms:

> May the Living One establish and support the work
>   of our hands
> and may the work of our hands establish the living
>   presence.
>
> —Psalm 90:17

Appendix I
Many Small Steps

With a few changes, this is the document I created on the "Bad Air Quality Day" (which I describe in chapter 1) shortly after my daughter was born. I started with small personal steps and then added more consumer activism and policy work toward the end. I see this as a natural progression from the personal to the public sphere. I called my new entity "Ecology Action Alliance."

Ecology Action Alliance is a network of individuals who are committed to making the changes—large and small—in our lifestyles that will allow us to live in a compatible way with the resources of our planet. There are no dues, there is no age limitation for membership. To become a member of EAA you must choose at least three "Small Steps" from this list to begin doing immediately. Add at least one step each week until you are living the most ecological lifestyle you can. You cannot join EAA on behalf of anyone else. Each of us must make our own commitment to the steps listed below.

STEPS TO REDUCE MY ECOLOGICAL FOOTPRINT

☐ I will recycle whatever I can through my municipality.

☐ I will buy snacks and other foods in degradable (paper) containers whenever possible.

☐ I will avoid buying/using clothing that requires dry cleaning.

☐ I will choose food and other products in the most ecological packaging available (paper, cotton, and glass as opposed to plastic).

☐ I will not buy/use Styrofoam products.

☐ I will not buy/use aerosol cans.

☐ I will start/expand my garden.

☐ I will reduce/eliminate toxic pesticides in my lawn and garden.

☐ I will purchase clean, renewable energy through my electric utility (www.gocleanenergy.com).

☐ I will join a gardening club.

☐ I will establish a bartering relationship with a neighbor (child care for knitting lessons?).

☐ I will set a radius (two blocks/two miles?) and make a commitment to walk everywhere I need to go within that radius.

☐ I will choose one day each week to refrain from driving.

☐ I will buy/repair/use a bicycle.

☐ I will make a serious and sustained effort to carpool and combine driving errands.

☐ I will patronize my neighborhood merchants.

☐ I will repair and reuse major appliances whenever possible.

☐ I will donate or find a use for items I no longer wish to use whenever possible (Volunteer Action Line of the United Way is a good source for recipients).

☐ I will patronize the used-goods market whenever possible.

☐ I will buy/utilize hand-powered appliances and tools whenever possible.

☐ I will become an urban livestock keeper (bees, eggs, poultry).

☐ I will copy this list and encourage one person each week to become a member of Ecology Action Alliance.

☐ I will share magazine subscriptions with friends or a library.

☐ I will reduce/eliminate toxic cleaning supplies and replace them with nonpoisonous cleaning supplies at my home/workplace.

☐ I will make a sustained effort to turn off appliances and lights that are not in use.

☐ I will encourage retailers and manufacturers to reduce/simplify packaging material.

☐ I will contract for a home energy audit (contact your utility company for details).

☐ I will use natural light and ventilation (windows!) whenever possible.

☐ I will encourage parents to use reusable supplies for diapering and washing their babies.

☐ I will use my/our children's "artwork" as stationery when writing to relatives.

☐ I will use simple measures (massage, tea, and rest) when dealing with common ailments.

☐ I will ask friends to consider natural products and materials when choosing gifts for me.

☐ I will order and use catalogues specializing in cotton clothing and natural materials.

☐ I will bring my own cloth or paper bags for shopping trips.

☐ I will eat the most wholesome and unadulterated diet possible.

☐ I will support businesses that promote environmental awareness.

☐ I will buy/request organic food at food stores and restaurants.

☐ I will join/contribute to an environmental group.

☐ I will buy/use recycled paper whenever possible.

☐ I will ask my grocer to carry local/organic produce.

☐ I will ask my grocer to carry alternatives to Styrofoam products.

☐ I will lobby my political representatives to make the environment a priority issue.

☐ I will petition my civic groups (school, business, congregation) to conserve, recycle, and consume responsibly.

☐ I will enjoy moments outside each day.

☐ I will learn about the vegetation and wildlife in my area.

☐ I will study and be a resource in my community for one aspect of the environmental agenda (solid waste, conservation, the charitable network, ecology legislation, whole foods, alternative healing, etc.).

APPENDIX II
CREATING A SUSTAINABLE CIVILIZATION
Joanna Macy's Theoretical Foundations

LISTED BELOW ARE THE THEORETICAL FOUNDATIONS that underscore the work of Joanna Macy. Joanna teaches all around the world, confronting and empowering others to engage with the great issues of our time, including conflict, nuclear proliferation, and ecology. I appreciate and use Joanna's work because it is spiritual but not theological. I have been able to communicate her ideas to adherents of many faith traditions because she seems to grasp a spiritual psychology that is shared beyond denominations. She calls her efforts the "Work That Reconnects."

THE GOALS OF THE WORK

The central purpose of the Work That Reconnects is to help people uncover and experience their innate connections with each other and with the systemic, self-healing powers in the web of life, so that they may be enlivened and motivated to play their part in creating a sustainable civilization…. The theory underlying this work … derives from the present challenge to choose life, from recognition of what stops us, and from understandings of the self-organizing power of the universe, the basic miracle. The following statements make more explicit the principles on which we base the Work That Reconnects.

150

THEORETICAL FOUNDATIONS

1. **This world, in which we are born and take our being, is *alive*.**
   It is not our supply house and sewer; it is our larger body. The intelligence that evolved us from stardust and interconnects us with all beings is sufficient for the healing of our earth community, if we but align with that purpose.

2. **Our true nature is far more ancient and encompassing than the separate self defined by habit and society.**
   We are as intrinsic to our living world as the rivers and trees, woven of the same intricate flows of matter/energy and mind. Having evolved us into self-reflexive consciousness, the world can now know itself through us, behold its own majesty, tell its own stories—and also respond to its own suffering.

3. **Our experience of pain for the world springs from our interconnectedness with all beings, from which also arises our powers to act on their behalf.**
   When we deny or repress our pain for the world, or treat it as a private pathology, our power to take part in the healing of our world is diminished. This apathy need not become a terminal condition. Our capacity to respond to our own and others' suffering—that is, the feedback loops that weave us into life—can be unblocked.

4. **Unblocking occurs when our pain for the world is not only intellectually validated, but experienced.**
   Cognitive information about the crises we face, or even about our psychological responses to them, is insufficient. We can only free ourselves from our fears of the pain—including the fear of getting permanently mired in despair or shattered by grief—when we allow ourselves to experience these feelings. Only then can we discover their fluid, dynamic character. Only then can they reveal on a visceral level our mutual belonging to the web of life.

151

5. **When we reconnect with life, by willingly enduring our pain for it, the mind retrieves its natural clarity.**

Not only do we experience our interconnectedness in the community of earth, but also mental eagerness arises to match this experience with new-paradigm thinking. Concepts that bring relatedness into focus become vivid. Significant learnings occur, for the individual system is reorganizing and reorienting, grounding itself in wider reaches of identity and self-interest.

6. **The experience of reconnection with the earth community arouses desire to act on its behalf.**

As earth's self-healing powers take hold within us, we feel called to participate in the Great Turning. For these self-healing powers to operate effectively, they must be trusted and acted on. The steps we take can be modest undertakings, but they should involve some risk to our mental comfort, lest we remain caught in old, "safe" limits. Courage is a great teacher and bringer of joy.

THOUGHTS FOR DISCUSSION AND ACTION
Format for an Eight-week Study Session

THIS STUDY GUIDE IS DESIGNED FOR A SMALL GROUP wanting to explore their perspective and role in creation care. The discussion questions are based on the assumption that group members will have read the chapter during the week prior to meeting, and that the group will meet for eight sessions. You could also use these questions for personal reflection.

It is not necessary to speak about all of the questions, but it is important to listen to each other well and share ideas about the questions that are most important to you. My hope is that the questions will help you continue the environmental conversation, and the work that needs to be done, beyond the pages of this book into your life and community. As Rev. Sally Bingham said so succinctly at the end of her Foreword, "We must all work together. It is the only way."

1 The Making of an Environmental Activist: Waking Up to the Problem

- What changes in the environment are getting your attention right now? What are your major concerns about the environmental crisis?

- What is your experience of recycling in your community? How well does it work? How well does it work in your home? Where would you like to do more?

- What do you consider to be the spiritual components of the environmental challenges we face?

- How you see your relationship to the trash mountain? What do you contribute? Do you think the problems of our excess trash are connected with our spiritual misalignment?

- What manifestations of global warming in your area have you noticed? Has it changed how you live?

- Where would you say you are in the five stages of grief (denial, anger, bargaining, depression, or acceptance) about global warming and why?

- How do you see your faith helping you become an agent of transformation for the environment?

- Take a look at the "Many Small Steps" list in the appendix. Choose three steps you could begin doing immediately. Then add one step each week until you are living the most ecological lifestyle you can. Why did you choose those three to start with?

2 The Makings of a Movement: The Interfaith Imperative and Its Obstacles

- What in your faith calls you to creation care? What are the "green roots" of your faith tradition?

- What advantages can you see in collaborating with people of other faiths on environmental issues? What might be the obstacles?

- What troubles you about interfaith efforts? What inspires you?

- How problematic do you think it would be for people in your faith to collaborate with people of other faiths? How does holding on to being "right" get in the way of being effective when working for the environment?

- What language of your faith do you think might be hardest for a person of another faith to accept? What language of another faith do you find hardest to accept? What language do you share in faith?

- What is your personal challenge in agreeing that "we are all in this together"?

- Which individual or group of another faith would you invite to engage in a discussion about creation care? What would you like to say to them? What do you need to hear from them?

- What influence can you imagine an interfaith environmental effort might have that people from your faith alone might not? What steps could you take toward connecting with people of other faiths on an environmental issue?

3 The New Wealth: Spirit Matters

- What does a rich life mean to you?

- How do you think the economy and the environment are related?

- What models of economy from biblical times do you think would help us today? What models from other countries or cultures would help us?

- What part(s) of Ezekiel's vision of dry bones resonates with you and why?

- What part of your faith calls you to the environmental table? What "urgings of the spirit" have you felt to become involved in environmental action?

- Who comprises your social wealth? In what ways is this more valuable to you than material wealth? How does your congregation support social wealth?

- What do you think of the idea that the pleasure of savoring deep, meaningful moments might do more to save the planet than hard sacrifice?

- What is your sense of corporate culture today? In what ways do you see yourself participating in it? Contributing to it? Rejecting it?

- Have you run into "green washing"? In what way? How can you let these companies know about your concerns?

- What alternatives can you imagine to change "business as usual" in your job or school or community? What about in your church or synagogue or mosque? What impact might this begin to have on your local environment?

4 Working Beyond Class and Race: Yes, We Do Need to Do This Together

- What would you say are the greatest environmental concerns in your community? How do environmental problems impact race and class in your town, or in the nearest city?

- What would your reaction be if you found out that a company wanted to build a pollution-generating business or a toxic chemical plant in your neighborhood? What would you try to do about it?

- Is your congregation race and income diverse? Are you or your congregation in partnership with congregations that are different from yours in these ways? If so, has that experience been enriching? Frustrating? Successful? If not, is this something you would suggest and why?

- Woody Bartlett affirms that to heal the planet, we must build long-term, individual relationships between people of differing class and race. Yet, at the same time, he admits it is not always comfortable. Where do you see yourself on this issue? What makes you uncomfortable? What motivates you to move forward?

- Which churches would you identify as the "ethnic churches" in your community? What environmental concerns do you think you share? How, and with whom, might you invite an open-ended inquiry into these concerns?

• What do you think are the links between environmental degradation and human misery, unemployment, violence, health, migration, and isolation? What are some of the ways you see environmental efforts as being able to support human dignity and safer communities?

• How might you get to the table of a group or church or organization of another race or class? Where could you show up?

• Where have you noticed someone of a different race or class doing something about the environmental concerns in your community? How might you connect with them to pool your energy and resources?

• Can you think of a mutual project you might work on together? What would be the first steps toward making this possible?

5 How Big Is Your God? Theology Meets Earth-Care Activism

• What do you believe about the relationship between God, humanity, and creation? How do you see or feel your relationship with the rest of creation?

• Where do you feel your interconnectedness with all of life? Do you have a moment to share about feeling alive in the living universe? Where were you? Can you recall the feeling now? How does that experience relate to your faith?

• Does your faith guide you in your environmental actions? How?

• Has your understanding of the universe, and the human place and purpose in it, changed over the years?

• What do you think of Rev. Tom Carr's idea that we are planetary creatures, first and foremost, that to harm the planet is to harm all beings that are alive here?

- What role do you think cataclysm might play in our current environmental crises, both in terms of destruction and of new life?

- Do you feel that we are trying to live above the earth and separate from nature? How has that affected us?

- How do you understand the phrase *in the end, all is one?*

- How do you think religion can compliment environmental stewardship? Do you think the environmental challenge can invigorate religion? How?

6 The New Eden: Reclaiming the Garden

- How many people do you know with food allergies? What are your concerns about food production in our country?

- Do you know any local farmers who have been affected by high-tech food production? What is being done in your area to support local foods? How might you help?

- Have you considered, or are you doing, organic gardening in your yard or community? What do you see as the advantages? How does your gardening open you to your connection with the earth? With your faith? What could you or your faith group do to support and encourage community gardens?

- Elisheva Rogosa says, "Loss of heritage wheats is a worldwide, silent crisis." What is your understanding of genetically modified foods? How important do you think it is to preserve heritage seeds? Are you aware of any local groups who are pursuing this? What might you do to become more involved?

- Andrea Ferich makes the statement that "the average American dinner plate of food travels 1,600 miles, and two-thirds of our domestic waste is food packaging." How much does this concern you? What steps could you take to change this in your neighborhood? At your local store?

- Andrea Ferich describes ways that they intercept children's decisions about buying junk food. What do you think you could do within your own family to influence your children's decisions?

- The simple acts of growing food and nourishing each other are basic to human life. How do you participate in this process? Where are you cut off from it? How is it a gain and how is it a loss to be separate from food production?

- How do you see seed saving as a model for eco-justice? How might you implement seed saving in your community?

7 • The New Sabbath: Less Is More

- How does your religion view the dichotomy between body versus soul? How do you experience this?

- Where do you see the relationship between spiritual hunger and material hunger in your life?

- What has your experience been of feeling closer to God in uncivilized places?

- How do you think our efforts to conquer nature have hurt us? How have they separated us from our Creator? What have we lost?

- How do you try to satisfy your hunger for awe?

- Where in your life do you think the phrase *less is more* is truly needed? What would be the potential rewards for you?

- Can you imagine designing a custom-made Sabbath? What might it look like? What might you do with the quiet, the freedom?

- Rev. Donna Schaper writes, "Before we save the world, we must remember to savor it." How do you see this as an important part of creation care? What might such a declaration mean in your own life?

- If you were to rate yourself on a giver-receiver scale of 1 to 10, with 1 being all giving and 10 being all receiving, where would you be? How might Sabbath time help you practice the art of receiving? How might a practice of resting in nature make you a better steward of nature?

- What new Sabbath rituals can you image creating that would contribute to making a smaller ecological footprint? How might you share these rituals with your religious community?

8 ⚭ Eco-Conversion: A New Paradigm for a New Earth

- If you were to look at your faith tradition with "green eyes," what would you see in its teachings about earth care? About consumption? About balance? About the interconnections between all life?

- What is your response to Rev. Margaret Bullitt-Jonas's question, "What needs to happen inside us in order for us to place care for the earth at the center of our moral and spiritual concern?"

- When in your life have you experienced what Bullitt-Jonas describes as The Creation Stage, falling in love with the beauty of God's creation?

- What might you need to change to honor the statement, "the first bit of nature with which you've been entrusted: your own body"?

- Where and how do you see The Crucifixion Stage—the assault on nature—taking place? How have you, or your church or community, been denying it? What do you need to mourn? What do you need to feel anger for?

- What are some ways you could enter The Resurrection Stage of eco-conversion, the stage of healing? Whom might you look to for support?

- What do you see as the role of prayer in eco-conversion?

- What witnesses have you seen for the care of the earth? How have these people's activism nourished a larger community?

- As you consider all that you've read in this book, what is your understanding of the environmental crisis as a manifestation of a spiritual problem?

- What is your hope for the immediate future? For the long-term future? How do you think your faith, along with the faith of others, can empower this to happen?

INTERFAITH ECOLOGICAL RESOURCES

THIS LIST OF RESOURCES is not intended to be comprehensive. It includes a smattering of materials, people, and links that I have found to be most helpful.

MEDIA

Lighten Up (DVD), available from The Regeneration Project (www.theregenerationproject.org), is an excellent adult education film on climate change and the faith imperative, hosted by Rev. Sally Bingham.

Renewal, a ninety-minute DVD documentary, is available from www.renewalproject.net. The DVD contains eight short vignettes on religious communities in action. The faith traditions represented are very diverse, and their projects include everything from paper recycling to coal mining and toxins. There is a short piece on an organic food co-op (Muslims) and outdoor education (Jewish). Very inspiring and easy to use for a variety of settings.

Affluenza, available from Bull Frog Films (www.bullfrogfilms.com/catalog/affl.html), is a fifty-six-minute film on the "disease of affluenza," which is caused by "consumerism, commercialism, and rampant materialism that is having a devastating impact on our families, communities, and the environment." Utterly serious and slightly lighthearted. Good for teens and adults. Show it before people do their Christmas and Hanukkah shopping!

WEBSITES

www.webofcreation.org has a collection of manuals and curricula. The work of Web of Creation is very spirited and ecumenical.

www.theregenerationproject.org coordinates the interfaith voice on climate change and the Interfaith Power and Light campaign. Most useful are the resources page (very rich and diverse) and the "Your State" page (faith-based networks in each state).

www.growseed.org is the home of the Heritage Wheat Conservancy and the work of Elisheva Rogosa, whose work is reported in this book (see chapter 6, "The New Eden"). This site offers curricula as well as seeds for growers who want to reclaim indigenous agriculture.

www.empowermentinstitute.net offers programs that are fun, intelligent, doable, and wise. Please check out this group, especially its Livable Neighborhood and Low Carbon Diet programs. This institute and all its trainings and books really put the *community* in community building, suggesting neighborhood and community-level projects, from street cleanups to local foraging.

fore.research.yale.edu is the website for the Forum on Religion and the Environment. FORE is an ambitious project to inspire the world's religions to pursue stewardship of the earth. FORE's conferences and gatherings inspire theological scholarship to frame environmental stewardship and prompt activism as well. I mention it here as an excellent compendium on each world religion's official resources on ecology and the environmental crisis.

PUBLICATIONS AND AUTHORS

Invoking the Spirit: Religion and Spirituality in the Quest for a Sustainable World is a paper by Gary Gardner that is available at www.worldwatch.org/node/826. *Invoking the Spirit* is a beautiful summary of the strengths in religious communities that make them an effective force for creation care.

Anne Rowthorn is a wonderful author whose books include words and images that truly touch and inspire. She gathers writers from many faith traditions who speak from the heart about wonder and life. *Earth and All the Stars: Reconnecting with Nature through Hymns, Stories, Poems, and Prayers from the World's Great Religions and Cultures* and *Song of the Universe: Earth Poems and Prose from Around the World* are full of liturgical-quality poems and short writings. See www.annerowthorn.com.

Amory Lovins is an upbeat and visionary scientist. My favorite quote of his is this: "Waste is an opportunity." He sees environmental innovation as a cornerstone of the future economy. His writings are hopeful, practical, and well informed. I especially enjoy *Natural Capitalism,* coauthored with Paul Hawken and L. Hunter Lovins.

Bill McKibben is another passionate and informed earth steward. His books are all rooted in his lived experience. Although his "highest level of religious official recognition was as a third-grade Sunday school teacher," there is a spiritual passion and lens to his writings. All his writings are challenging, truthful, and eye-opening. See www.billmckibben.com/books.html.

Animal Vegetable Miracle: A Year of Food Life is a book on food simplicity by Barbara Kingsolver. In this finely observed book, she describes the experience of becoming a "local-vore"; that is, eating locally grown foods for a year. Her website generously includes recipes. See www.animalvegetablemiracle.com.

Matthew Fox is a writer and teacher and so much more. He has been reclaiming a joyful relationship with creation for decades and is a founder of the Creation Spirituality movement. This movement seeds the philosophy and community-organizing principles to help us evolve new, more joyful and sustainable communities. See www.matthewfox.org for his writings and events.

50 Simple Things You Can Do to Save the Earth by John, Sophie, and Jesse Javna is an update of the 1990 classic. This book is more than a list; it is an action plan for deeper, more transformative steps. The authors include a tremendous listing of resource people, groups, and writings to supplement each of their chapters. Topics include green building, energy, transportation, food, and fair trade—all the biggies. Seewww.50simplethings.com.

Joanna Macy is one of my favorite authors in this field. She has worked as a peace and anti-nuclear proliferation activist. The overarching scariness of nuclear annihilation led her to observe how we are capable of shutting down in the face of global challenges. Her book *Coming Back to Life: Practices to Reconnect Our Lives, Our World*, coauthored with Molly Young Brown, is a beautiful collection of philosophy, psychology, inspired stories, and rituals to help us do this reconnecting. Her book is very user-friendly, and the rituals are powerful, simple, and easy to facilitate, even though the material is subtle and profound. This book is a good resource for earth ministry and powerful worship, although it is nondenominational. See www.joannamacy.net. (Joanna and her publisher have graciously given permission for her "Theoretical Foundations" to be included in this book. See page 151).

Love God, Heal Earth: 21 Leading Religious Voices Speak Out on Our Sacred Duty to Protect the Environment, collated by Rev. Sally Bingham, is a gathering of voices, each speaking from deep within their religious identity. The contributors have found ways to see the green roots of their faith commitments. If you order through The Regeneration Project (www.theregenerationproject.org), a portion of your purchase supports the Interfaith Power and Light affiliates.

The Hand of God: A Collection of Thoughts and Images Reflecting the Spirit of the Universe is a stunning book by Sharon Begley. It is edited by Michael Reagan, principal of Lionheart Books. Although currently available in the UK, it is a little harder to track down in the United States, but it is well worth the effort. The visual images in this book will bring home the point about how startlingly beautiful this cosmos is. It will make you feel small and enormous at the same time.

Putting Energy into Stewardship: An Energy Star Guide for Congregations is a publication of the U.S. Environmental Pro-tection Agency and can be downloaded online at www. energystar.gov/ia/business/small_business/congregations_ guidebook/Cong_Guide.pdf. This book, together with a small group of congregants (at least one of whom is comfortable with a toolbelt), can make a big difference in a congregation's energy consumption. The document is practical, empowering, and well organized.

To Serve Christ in All Creation is an example of a denominational study guide for congregations on the subject of stewardship. It was created for the Connecticut Diocese of the Episcopal Church and can be downloaded online at www.ctdiocese.org/images/ customer-files/environment.pdf.

RETREAT CENTERS

Going to a residential center for a retreat is a popular way to immerse oneself in a natural environment and a "whole body" way of learning. There are centers around the country that share their knowledge about tracking local flora and fauna, gardening, and the philosophy of deep ecology. Often these centers have very knowl-edgeable staff on site and host retreats with some of the folks men-tioned in this book and other leaders in the field.

The Catholic world has a long history of residential community. There are several Catholic farms and retreat centers that incorporate cutting-edge green technology, theology, and living. But most denominational retreat centers and most religious camps for youth are incorporating natural education into their programming for all ages. I have listed below a small sampling of retreat centers that I have had some contact with and a few intriguing-looking places that I came across during a Web search.

Genesis Farm in Blairstown, New Jersey, is a learning center for earth studies. Here, facilitators practice and teach gardening, earth literacy, and deeply religious ecology. Cofounder Sister Miriam MacGillis has been an influential voice for earth stewardship for two generations. Treat yourself to one of Genesis's weeklong trainings. See www.genesisfarm.org.

Ignatius Jesuit Center in Guelph, Canada, has a well-envisioned program of ecology studies in a faith idiom. See www. ignatiusguelph.ca/ ecology/eco_contact.html.

Star Island has summer programming for all ages. Several denominations, notably Unitarians and Church of Christ/Congregationalists, use this beautiful site off the coast of Maine for regular retreats. See www.starisland.org.

Pendle Hill is a Quaker retreat in Wallingford, Pennsylvania, with year-round programming for all ages. It offers a rich mix of integrated retreats, bringing together body and heart, world and self, spirit and action. See www.pendlehill.org.

Au Sable Institute has campuses in Michigan and Washington State and year-round programs for all ages, including college-accredited studies. Their stated mission is "the integration of knowledge of the creation with biblical principles for the purpose of bringing the Christian community and the general public to a better understanding of the Creator and the stewardship of God's creation." See www.ausable.org/au.main.cfm.

Isabella Freedman Jewish Retreat Center in Falls Village, Connecticut, offers year-round programming for Jewish youth, families, and adults in many areas, including sustainability and agriculture. See www.isabellafreedman.org.

ACKNOWLEDGMENTS

I AM VERY GRATEFUL for the opportunity to share with you the wise teaching of my many colleagues in what Thomas Berry calls the "Great Work." My personal thanks go to the authors who contributed their profound writing and thoughts to this volume and to the many teachers and friends whose wise words are quoted in it.

I wish to acknowledge the coordinators of the annual Call to Action conference, which brings together Catholics and fellow travelers "working together to foster peace and justice." Their invitation to me to address their gathering in 2007 and 2008 became the seed for this work.

This book would not exist without the deep heart and good eye of my editor at SkyLight Paths, Marcia Broucek. Marcia heard my talks at Call to Action; she heard in them a message she wished others to hear. She reflected back to me, at every stage of the work, what was vital, what was new, and what was the best way to communicate it. I am very grateful for her many skills and her deep appreciation of the message.

The entire team at SkyLight Paths has been enthusiastic and supportive. I am grateful for their tremendous vision and their supportive professional culture.

I am grateful to the people of my spiritual home, Congregation Pnai Or of Central Connecticut. The loving people of this community have been cocreators of much of my social wealth.

And finally, I am grateful to you, the reader, who is willing to tolerate what you feel and what you know on behalf of the work. So much is at stake; it is all so precious and irreplaceable. I am grateful to all who widen their hearts to feel the sorrow, the resolve, and the commitment to heal.

ABOUT THE CONTRIBUTORS

Rev. Woody Bartlett, a retired Episcopal priest living in Atlanta, is the cofounder and chair of the board of Georgia Interfaith Power and Light (GIPL). GIPL works with communities of faith to be effective stewards of God's creation through the sustainable generation and efficient use of energy. In addition to working with GIPL, Woody is active in the development of public policy pertaining to energy efficiency and green energy. He is also on the Environmental Stewardship Task Force of the Episcopal Diocese of Atlanta, a group that is also engaging its churches to be better stewards of creation. Recently, he has been elected to the board of The Regeneration Project, the national sponsor of the Interfaith Power and Light movement. Woody is also the author of *Living by Surprise: A Christian Response to the Ecological Crisis.*

Rev. Sally Bingham is a priest in the Diocese of California and cochair of the Episcopal Diocesan Commission for the Environment. She is also founder and president of The Regeneration Project, whose Interfaith Power and Light (IPL) campaign is a religious response to global warming. The IPL campaign includes a national network of more than five thousand congregations with affiliated programs in twenty-nine states. Sally has been active in the environmental community for more than twenty-five years, bringing widespread recognition to the link between faith and the environment. As one of the first faith leaders to fully recognize global warming as a moral issue, she has mobilized thousands of religious people to put their faith into action through energy stewardship and advocacy. Sally currently serves on both the national board of the Environmental Defense Fund and the Environmental Working Group, as well as the national advisory board for the Union of Concerned Scientists. In October 2008, *Grist* magazine named her as one of the top fifteen green religious leaders.

Rev. Margaret Bullitt-Jonas, PhD, is priest associate of Grace (Episcopal) Church in Amherst, Massachusetts, and serves on the Leadership Council of Religious Witness for the Earth, an interfaith network dedicated to public witness in defense of creation. She has been active in the Leadership Council since her arrest in 2001 during an interfaith prayer vigil at the Department of Energy in Washington, D.C., to protest oil drilling in the Arctic. Margaret is the author of *Holy Hunger* and *Christ's Passion, Our Passions*, and the principal author of "To Serve Christ in All Creation: A Pastoral Letter from the Episcopal Bishops of New England." A retreat leader and spiritual director, Margaret served for several years as chaplain to the bishops of the Episcopal Church. She is currently writing her next book, which has as its working title *Love Every Leaf: Spiritual Memoir of an Eco-Activist*.

Rev. Tom Carr is the senior minister of the First Baptist Church of West Hartford, Connecticut, and is the cofounder of the Interreligious Eco-Justice Network, Connecticut's Interfaith Power and Light. IREJN/CIPL works with congregations of diverse faith traditions in education, advocacy, and the celebration of the sacredness of creation, encouraging faithful living that supports a sustainable relationship between humankind and the environment. For more than twenty years, Tom has been involved in issues of ecology and environmental justice with churches and through interfaith relations. He serves as the American Baptist Churches of Connecticut eco-justice coordinator, was part of the National

Council of Churches Eco-Justice Working Group, and is the cofounder of the interfaith Earth Prayers. An ordained American Baptist pastor, Tom also preaches, offers workshops, and works with religious communities to help them understand their particular faith tradition's role in caring for the earth and all of God's creation. His current interests involve exploring Christianity within the new cosmology.

Mohamad A. Chakaki is an environmental consultant with the Baraka Group on environmental and community development projects in the United States and the Middle East. He is also an active member of two environmental networks in the Washington, D.C., area—the Greater Washington Interfaith Power and Light (GWIPL) and DC Green Muslims. His passion for nature and people has led him to work in parks and gardens across the United States, in Central Africa through the Peace Corps, and in Syria (with the United Nations). Mohamad holds a master's degree in urban ecology and environmental design from Yale University and undergraduate degrees in religion and biology from George Washington University. He was interviewed for his perspective, and his comments appear throughout the book.

Andrea Ferich lives, works, and worships in Camden, New Jersey, at Sacred Heart Church. As a farmer and greenhouse manager, she runs a four-season harvest and seed-to-table program at Eve's Garden through the Heart of Camden (www.heartofcamden.org). She is also a cofounder of the Camden Community House and continues to develop the ecological liturgy through the Center for Transformation (www.camdencenterfortransformation.org), an environmental justice retreat center in Camden. She studied ecological economics at Eastern University and recently received the Delaware Valley Environmental Leadership Program Fellowship. When her hands are not in the earth, she most thoroughly enjoys kite flying, bird-watching, and paddling downstream.

Eboo Patel is the founder and executive director of the Interfaith Youth Core, a Chicago-based international nonprofit organization working to build mutual respect and pluralism among religiously diverse young people by empowering them to work together to serve others. He is the author of *Acts of Faith: The Story of an American Muslim, the Struggle for the Soul of a Generation* and writes "The Faith Divide," a featured blog on religion for the *Washington Post*. Eboo holds a doctorate in the sociology of religion from Oxford University, where he studied on a Rhodes scholarship, and is an Ashoka Fellow, part of a select group of social entrepreneurs whose ideas are changing the world. He has been named by *Islamica Magazine* as one of ten young Muslim visionaries shaping Islam in America. He was interviewed for his perspective, and his comments appear throughout the book.

Dr. Lowell "Rusty" Pritchard is a resource economist, and since 2006 he has been the national director of outreach for the Evangelical Environmental Network (EEN) and the editor of *Creation Care* magazine, a Christian environmental quarterly. Prior to coming to EEN, he was a full-time faculty member in environmental studies at Emory University; he helped create that program in 1999 and maintains an adjunct affiliation. Rusty holds degrees from Duke University (BS, zoology) and the University of Florida (PhD, resource economics; MS, environmental engineering sciences), and has taught courses in natural resource economics, environmental institutions, public health, resource use and management, environmental justice, ecological economics, and environmental decision making under uncertain conditions. Rusty currently lives in inner-city Atlanta with his wife and three children, where they serve in a multiracial church doing church development, neighborhood evangelism, and community development.

Elisheva Rogosa is the principal investigator for Northeast Organic Wheat, a USDA-funded consortium of organic farmers and artisan bakers working together to cultivate ancient wheats in the Northeast, and Nourishing Peace, a cooperation of Arab and Jewish seed savers in Israel and Palestine. She is also the founding director of the Heritage Wheat Conservancy, whose mission is to replenish and distribute ancient indigenous wheat varieties (see www.growseed.org).

Rev. Donna Schaper, PhD, is senior minister of Judson Memorial Church in New York City and the principal of Bricks Without Straw Consulting Service, which helps nonprofits and congregations raise funds, use conflict creatively, and do a lot with a little. The author of *Sabbath Keeping,* her two newest books are *Doing Good While Living Well* and *Grass Roots Gardening: Rituals to Sustain Activism.* Her blog guides social activists to create nourishing spiritual practices so their work in the world can be sustained and balanced; it can be found at DollyMama@wordpress.com. She also blogs on the *Huffington Post* and for the *Progressive Christian.*

CREDITS

The Foreword by Rev. Sally Bingham is printed with permission.

The author's interview with Dr. Lowell "Rusty" Pritchard in chapter 2 has been published in a more complete form, "Sharing the Earth," in *Sh'ma: A Journal of Jewish Responsibility*, June 2008. The conversation appeared as part of an issue exploring Judaism and the environment. Reprinted with permission from *Sh'ma: A Journal of Jewish Responsibility* (www.shma.com).

The interview with Mohamad A. Chakaki is printed with permission.

The Great Light Bulb Swap of '06: Working Beyond Class and Race by Rev. Woody Bartlett is reprinted with permission.

The Big Context by Rev. Tom Carr is reprinted with permission.

Alumot by Elisheva Rogosa is reprinted with permission.

Communion Agriculture: Eve's Garden by Andrea Ferich is reprinted with permission.

Green Sabbath by Rev. Donna Schaper, PhD, is reprinted with permission.

"Conversion to Eco-Justice" by Rev. Margaret Bullitt-Jonas in chapter 8 is an excerpt adapted from the author's chapter, published in *Earth and Word: Classic Sermons on Saving the Planet*, ed. David Rhoads. Copyright © 2007 by David Rhoads. Reprinted by permission of The Continuum International Publishing Group.

The eco-conversion on p. 138–139 by Lynn Fulkerson is printed with permission.

The interview with Eboo Patel is printed with permission.

Joanna Macy's "Theoretical Foundations," from *Coming Back to Life: Practices to Reconnect Our Lives, Our World* (coauthored with Molly Young Brown), pp. 59–60, copyright © 1998 by Joanna R. Macy and Molly Young Brown, are reprinted with permission from Joanna Macy and New Society Press.

Global Spiritual Perspectives

Spiritual Perspectives on America's Role as Superpower
by the Editors at SkyLight Paths

Are we the world's good neighbor or a global bully? From a spiritual perspective, what are America's responsibilities as the only remaining superpower? Contributors:

Dr. Beatrice Bruteau • Dr. Joan Brown Campbell • Tony Campolo • Rev. Forrest Church • Lama Surya Das • Matthew Fox • Kabir Helminski • Thich Nhat Hanh • Eboo Patel • Abbot M. Basil Pennington, ocso • Dennis Prager • Rosemary Radford Ruether • Wayne Teasdale • Rev. William McD. Tully • Rabbi Arthur Waskow • John Wilson

5½ x 8½, 256 pp, Quality PB, 978-1-893361-81-2 **$16.95**

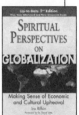

Spiritual Perspectives on Globalization, 2nd Edition
Making Sense of Economic and Cultural Upheaval
by Ira Rifkin; Foreword by Dr. David Little, Harvard Divinity School

What is globalization? Surveys the religious landscape. Includes a new Discussion Guide designed for group use.

5½ x 8½, 256 pp, Quality PB, 978-1-59473-045-0 **$16.99**

Native American

Native American Stories of the Sacred: Annotated & Explained
Retold & Annotated by Evan T. Pritchard

Intended for more than entertainment, these teaching tales contain elegantly simple illustrations of time-honored truths.

5½ x 8½, 272 pp, Quality PB, 978-1-59473-112-9 **$16.99**

Children's Spirituality

In Our Image: God's First Creatures
by Nancy Sohn Swartz; Full-color illus. by Melanie Hall

A playful new twist on the Genesis story—from the perspective of the animals. Celebrates the interconnectedness of nature and the harmony of all living things.

9 x 12, 32 pp, HC, Full-color illus., 978-1-879045-99-6 **$16.95**
For ages 4 & up (A book from Jewish Lights, SkyLight Paths' sister imprint)

Noah's Wife: The Story of Naamah
by Sandy Eisenberg Sasso; Full-color illus. by Bethanne Andersen

This new story, based on an ancient text, opens readers' religious imaginations to new ideas about the well-known story of the Flood. When God tells Noah to bring the animals of the world onto the ark, God also calls on Naamah, Noah's wife, to save each plant on Earth.

9 x 12, 32 pp, HC, Full-color illus., 978-1-58023-134-3 **$16.95**
For ages 4 & up (A book from Jewish Lights, SkyLight Paths' sister imprint)

Also available: **Naamah:** Noah's Wife (A Board Book)
by Sandy Eisenberg Sasso; Full-color illus. by Bethanne Andersen
5 x 5, 24 pp, Board Book, Full-color illus., 978-1-893361-56-0 **$7.99** *For ages 0–4*

Or phone, fax, mail or e-mail to: SKYLIGHT PATHS Publishing
Sunset Farm Offices, Route 4 • P.O. Box 237 • Woodstock, Vermont 05091
Tel: (802) 457-4000 • Fax: (802) 457-4004 • www.skylightpaths.com
Credit card orders: (800) 962-4544 (8:30AM–5:30PM ET Monday–Friday)
Generous discounts on quantity orders. SATISFACTION GUARANTEED. Prices subject to change.

Spirituality & Crafts

Contemplative Crochet: A Hands-On Guide for Interlocking Faith and Craft *by Cindy Crandall-Frazier; Foreword by Linda Skolnik*
Illuminates the spiritual lessons you can learn through crocheting.
7 x 9, 208 pp, b/w photographs, Quality PB, 978-1-59473-238-6 **$16.99**

The Knitting Way: A Guide to Spiritual Self-Discovery
by Linda Skolnik and Janice MacDaniels
Examines how you can explore and strengthen your spiritual life through knitting.
7 x 9, 240 pp, b/w photographs, Quality PB, 978-1-59473-079-5 **$16.99**

The Painting Path: Embodying Spiritual Discovery through Yoga, Brush and Color *by Linda Novick; Foreword by Richard Segalman*
Explores the divine connection you can experience through creativity.
7 x 9, 208 pp, 8-page full-color insert, plus b/w photographs
Quality PB, 978-1-59473-226-3 **$18.99**

The Quilting Path: A Guide to Spiritual Discovery through Fabric, Thread and Kabbalah *by Louise Silk*
Explores how to cultivate personal growth through quilt making.
7 x 9, 192 pp, b/w photographs and illustrations, Quality PB, 978-1-59473-206-5 **$16.99**

The Scrapbooking Journey: A Hands-On Guide to Spiritual Discovery
by Cory Richardson-Lauve; Foreword by Stacy Julian
Reveals how this craft can become a practice used to deepen and shape your life.
7 x 9, 176 pp, 8-page full-color insert, plus b/w photographs, Quality PB, 978-1-59473-216-4 **$18.99**

The Soulwork of Clay: A Hands-On Approach to Spirituality
by Marjory Zoet Bankson; Photographs by Peter Bankson
Takes you through the seven-step process of making clay into a pot, drawing parallels at each stage to the process of spiritual growth.
7 x 9, 192 pp, b/w photographs, Quality PB, 978-1-59473-249-2 **$16.99**

Religious Etiquette / Reference

How to Be a Perfect Stranger, 4th Edition: The Essential Religious Etiquette Handbook *Edited by Stuart M. Matlins and Arthur J. Magida*
The indispensable guidebook to help the well-meaning guest when visiting other people's religious ceremonies. A straightforward guide to the rituals and celebrations of the major religions and denominations in the United States and Canada from the perspective of an interested guest of any other faith, based on information obtained from authorities of each religion. Belongs in every living room, library and office. Covers:

African American Methodist Churches • Assemblies of God • Bahá'í • Baptist • Buddhist • Christian Church (Disciples of Christ) • Christian Science (Church of Christ, Scientist) • Churches of Christ • Episcopalian and Anglican • Hindu • Islam • Jehovah's Witnesses • Jewish • Lutheran • Mennonite/Amish • Methodist • Mormon (Church of Jesus Christ of Latter-day Saints) • Native American/First Nations • Orthodox Churches • Pentecostal Church of God • Presbyterian • Quaker (Religious Society of Friends) • Reformed Church in America/Canada • Roman Catholic • Seventh-day Adventist • Sikh • Unitarian Universalist • United Church of Canada • United Church of Christ
6 x 9, 432 pp, Quality PB, 978-1-59473-140-2 **$19.99**

The Perfect Stranger's Guide to Funerals and Grieving Practices: A Guide to Etiquette in Other People's Religious Ceremonies *Edited by Stuart M. Matlins*
6 x 9, 240 pp, Quality PB, 978-1-893361-20-1 **$16.95**

The Perfect Stranger's Guide to Wedding Ceremonies: A Guide to Etiquette in Other People's Religious Ceremonies *Edited by Stuart M. Matlins*
6 x 9, 208 pp, Quality PB, 978-1-893361-19-5 **$16.95**

Spirituality of the Seasons

Autumn: A Spiritual Biography of the Season
Edited by Gary Schmidt and Susan M. Felch; Illustrations by Mary Azarian
Rejoice in autumn as a time of preparation and reflection. Includes Wendell Berry, David James Duncan, Robert Frost, A. Bartlett Giamatti, E. B. White, P. D. James, Julian of Norwich, Garret Keizer, Tracy Kidder, Anne Lamott, May Sarton.
6 x 9, 320 pp, 5 b/w illus., Quality PB, 978-1-59473-118-1 **$18.99**

Spring: A Spiritual Biography of the Season
Edited by Gary Schmidt and Susan M. Felch; Illustrations by Mary Azarian
Explore the gentle unfurling of spring and reflect on how nature celebrates rebirth and renewal. Includes Jane Kenyon, Lucy Larcom, Harry Thurston, Nathaniel Hawthorne, Noel Perrin, Annie Dillard, Martha Ballard, Barbara Kingsolver, Dorothy Wordsworth, Donald Hall, David Brill, Lionel Basney, Isak Dinesen, Paul Laurence Dunbar. 6 x 9, 352 pp, 6 b/w illus., Quality PB, 978-1-59473-246-1 **$18.99**

Summer: A Spiritual Biography of the Season
Edited by Gary Schmidt and Susan M. Felch; Illustrations by Barry Moser
"A sumptuous banquet.... These selections lift up an exquisite wholeness found within an everyday sophistication."— ★ *Publishers Weekly* starred review
Includes Anne Lamott, Luci Shaw, Ray Bradbury, Richard Selzer, Thomas Lynch, Walt Whitman, Carl Sandburg, Sherman Alexie, Madeleine L'Engle, Jamaica Kincaid.
6 x 9, 304 pp, 5 b/w illus., Quality PB, 978-1-59473-183-9 **$18.99**
HC, 978-1-59473-083-2 **$21.99**

Winter: A Spiritual Biography of the Season
Edited by Gary Schmidt and Susan M. Felch; Illustrations by Barry Moser
"This outstanding anthology features top-flight nature and spirituality writers on the fierce, inexorable season of winter.... Remarkably lively and warm, despite the icy subject." — ★ *Publishers Weekly* starred review
6 x 9, 288 pp, 6 b/w illus., Deluxe PB w/flaps, 978-1-893361-92-8 **$18.95**

Spirituality / Animal Companions

Blessing the Animals: Prayers and Ceremonies to Celebrate God's Creatures, Wild and Tame *Edited by Lynn L. Caruso*
5¼ x 7¼, 256 pp, Quality PB, 978-1-59473-253-9 **$15.99**; HC, 978-1-59473-145-7 **$19.99**

Remembering My Pet: A Kid's Own Spiritual Workbook for When a Pet Dies
by Nechama Liss-Levinson, PhD, and Rev. Molly Phinney Baskette, MDiv; Foreword by Lynn L. Caruso
8 x 10, 48 pp, 2-color text, HC, 978-1-59473-221-3 **$16.99**

What Animals Can Teach Us about Spirituality: Inspiring Lessons from Wild and Tame Creatures *by Diana L. Guerrero* 6 x 9, 176 pp, Quality PB, 978-1-893361-84-3 **$16.95**

Spirituality

Next to Godliness: Finding the Sacred in Housekeeping
Edited and with Introductions by Alice Peck
Offers new perspectives on how we can reach out for the Divine.
6 x 9, 224 pp, Quality PB, 978-1-59473-214-0 **$19.99**

Bread, Body, Spirit: Finding the Sacred in Food
Edited and with Introductions by Alice Peck
Explores how food feeds our faith. 6 x 9, 224 pp, Quality PB, 978-1-59473-242-3 **$19.99**

Renewal in the Wilderness: A Spiritual Guide to Connecting with God in the Natural World *by John Lionberger*
Reveals the power of experiencing God's presence in many variations of the natural world. 6 x 9, 176 pp, b/w photos, Quality PB, 978-1-59473-219-5 **$16.99**

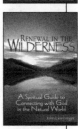

Journeys of Simplicity: Traveling Light with Thomas Merton, Bashō, Edward Abbey, Annie Dillard & Others *by Philip Harnden*
5 x 7¼, 144 pp, Quality PB, 978-1-59473-181-5 **$12.99** 128 pp, HC, 978-1-893361-76-8 **$16.95**

About SKYLIGHT PATHS Publishing

SkyLight Paths Publishing is creating a place where people of different spiritual traditions come together for challenge and inspiration, a place where we can help each other understand the mystery that lies at the heart of our existence.

Through spirituality, our religious beliefs are increasingly becoming a part of our lives—rather than *apart* from our lives. While many of us may be more interested than ever in spiritual growth, we may be less firmly planted in traditional religion. Yet, we do want to deepen our relationship to the sacred, to learn from our own as well as from other faith traditions, and to practice in new ways.

SkyLight Paths sees both believers and seekers as a community that increasingly transcends traditional boundaries of religion and denomination—people wanting to learn from each other, *walking together, finding the way.*

For your information and convenience, at the back of this book we have provided a list of other SkyLight Paths books you might find interesting and useful. They cover the following subjects:

Buddhism / Zen	Global Spiritual	Monasticism
Catholicism	Perspectives	Mysticism
Children's Books	Gnosticism	Poetry
Christianity	Hinduism /	Prayer
Comparative	Vedanta	Religious Etiquette
Religion	Inspiration	Retirement
Current Events	Islam / Sufism	Spiritual Biography
Earth-Based	Judaism	Spiritual Direction
Spirituality	Kabbalah	Spirituality
Enneagram	Meditation	Women's Interest
	Midrash Fiction	Worship